MW00445314

DISCOVERING THE SEER IN YOU

Books by James W. Goll

Intercession: The Power and Passion to Shape History
James W. Goll 365-Day Personal Prayer Guide
Prayer Storm
Prayer Storm Study Guide
Shifting Shadows of Supernatural Experiences
The Call of the Elijah Revolution
The Seer
The Seer Devotional Journal
The Lost Art of Intercession
The Lost Art of Practicing His Presence

Books by James W. Goll and Michal Ann Goll

Angelic Encounters
Compassion: A Call to Take Action
Dream Language: The Prophetic Power of Dreams, Revelations, and the Spirit of Wisdom
God Encounters
Call to the Secret Place
Women on the Frontlines: A Call to Courage

AVAILABLE FROM DESTINY IMAGE PUBLISHERS

DISCOVERING THE SEER IN YOU

EXPLORING YOUR PROPHETIC GIFTS

JAMES W. GOLL

© Copyright 2007—Encounters Network

All rights reserved. This book is protected by the copyright laws of the United States of America. This book may not be copied or reprinted for commercial gain or profit. The use of short quotations or occasional page copying for personal or group study is permitted and encouraged. Permission will be granted upon request. Unless otherwise indicated, Scripture is taken from the NEW AMERICAN STANDARD BIBLE®, Copyright © 1960, 1962, 1963, 1968, 1971, 1972, 1973, 1975, 1977, 1995 by The Lockman Foundation. Used by permission. Scriptures marked NIV are taken from the HOLY BIBLE, NEW INTERNATIONAL VERSION®, Copyright © 1973, 1978, 1984 by the International Bible Society. Used by permission of Zondervan. All rights reserved. Scriptures marked NKJV are taken from the New King James Version®, Copyright © 1982 by Thomas Nelson, Inc. Used by permission. All rights reserved. Scriptures marked KJV are taken from the King James Version. Please note that Destiny Image's publishing style capitalizes certain pronouns in Scripture that refer to the Father, Son, and Holy Spirit, and may differ from some publishers' styles. Take note that the name satan and related names are not capitalized. We choose not to acknowledge him, even to the point of violating grammatical rules.

DESTINY IMAGE® PUBLISHERS, INC.
P.O. Box 310, Shippensburg, PA 17257-0310

"Promoting Inspired Lives"

This book and all other Destiny Image, Revival Press, Mercy Place, Fresh Bread, Destiny Image Fiction, and Treasure House books are available at Christian bookstores and distributors worldwide.

For a U.S. bookstore nearest you, call 1-800-722-6774.
For more information on foreign distributors, call 717-532-3040.
Or reach us on the Internet: www.destinyimage.com

Previously Published by Encounters Network ~ a ministry to the nations
P.O. Box 1653, Franklin, TN 37065

ISBN 10: 0-7684-2743-6
ISBN 13: 978-0-7684-2743-1

For Worldwide Distribution, Printed in the U.S.A.
5 6 7 8 9 10 11 / 16 15 14 13 12

DEDICATION

I wish to dedicate this study guide in honor of two fathers who have immensely impacted my journey. They are each unique seers in this era of Christianity: John Sandford and Bob Jones. I am grateful to the Lord for these fatherly seers who have pioneered a way for the next generation of eagles to arise and fly!

ENDORSEMENTS

for *The Seer*

Jim Goll has blessed the Body of Christ with a greater understanding of the prophetic voice of the Lord. He has given much biblical insight and personal experience that helps us understand the unique ministry of the Prophet and the Seer. Also, valuable guidelines and principles are given concerning how to discern a true word from the Lord and how to properly minister that word. This book will be a very valuable resource for those who desire to be used in prophetic ministry.

Dr. Bill Hamon
Chairman and Founder, Christian International
Author, *Apostles, Prophets and the Coming Move of God*

James Goll's book *The Seer* is long overdue. Few can or do write like him. He blends a rare combination of being both scholarly and very inspiring. It's fascinating to me that though I operate prophetically, it has been the seers in my life, sent by God, who have given me the most significant revelation and direction for the ministry of The Elijah List, as well as keeping me in touch with the plans of God for my life.

Steve Shultz, The Elijah List
www.elijahlist.com

Jim Goll's profound work *The Seer*, is an excellent tool to educate the Church on the gift of foresight and its significance in the lives of God's people. The principles shared in this book will address misconceptions about "seeing" and prepare the reader to experience the awesome benefits of this ministry. I highly recommend *The Seer* to those who desire to know "what is yet to come."

Dr. Kingsley A. Fletcher
International Speaker, Government Advisor, Author and Pastor
Research Triangle Park, North Carolina

For all those who are seers and have wondered if anyone understood you, this book is a gift for you. Jim Goll has clearly and scripturally opened the way for the seer gift to be used in the Body of Christ. Fascinating book! You will love it!

Cindy Jacobs
Generals of Intercession

Navigating the unseen realm can be both enticing and challenging as believers seek to grow deeper in the gifts of the Spirit, particularly related to that of the seer gifting. Enticing, because it is awe-inspiring to come in contact with the power and presence of the Lord through spiritual experiences that are often part of that gifting. Challenging, because it is critical that the Word of God and spiritual disciplines such as prayer and intimacy remain the solid footing on which revelational experiences are interpreted.

Jim Goll has succeeded in presenting a comprehensive study of the prophet/seer gift sharing substantial biblical understanding as well as experience from his own spiritual journey. As with Jim's previous books, this one could well become a manual for those pursuing the seer anointing.

Jane Hansen
President, Aglow International

If all you have is the Spirit, you can blow up, but if you have the Spirit and the Word, you will grow up. Nowhere have I found that adage more amply and wisely elucidated than in Jim Goll's *The Seer*.

Jim couples breathtaking revelation with wisdom, piercing insight with discretion, high spirituality with balance and accountability, new knowledge and understanding with exciting mystical experience.

The Seer is a boat to shoot over the dangerous rocks of the rapids into the high seas of prophetic expression and fruitfulness in the Lord. Having pioneered the modern prophetic movement almost thirty years ago with the book, *The Elijah Task*, I find in Jim's book *The Seer* a most worthy successor. To me, it is an honor to recommend this book to all. My hope and prayer is that you will not just read it, but live it to the max for the glory of our Lord.

John Sandford
Co-founder, Elijah House International
Author, *The Elijah Task*

TABLE OF
CONTENTS

INSTRUCTIONAL GUIDELINES AND REFERENCE MATERIALS

The following study guide has been prepared especially for you by James W. Goll. The lessons are tailor-made with your individual, small group, or training center needs in mind. At the end of each lesson, there are Reflective Questions to help you in your review of the materials you have studied. The answers can be found in the back of this study guide.

This study guide directly corresponds with the book *The Seer*, published by Destiny Image, with each of the 12 lessons in this study guide relating directly to the 12 chapters in *The Seer*:

Section One: Understanding the Seer Realm
Chapter One: Seer and Prophet: Two Prophetic Streams
Chapter Two: Dimensions of the Prophetic Anointing
Chapter Three: Vision: The Power That Sustains
Chapter Four: The Diversity of Visionary States

Section Two: Spiritual Discernment
Chapter Five: Wisely Judging Revelatory Encounters
Chapter Six: Discerning of Spirits

Section Three: Dreams, Visions, and Other Heavenly Realms
Chapter Seven: Dream Language
Chapter Eight: Levels of Supernatural Visions
Chapter Nine: The Ecstatic Realms of the Spirit

Section Four: Intimacy: The Goal of All Things
Chapter Ten: Standing in the Council of God
Chapter Eleven: Hidden Streams of the Prophetic
Chapter Twelve: The Key of Intimacy to Open Heavens

PREFACE

Every born-again believer has two sets of eyes. We have our physical eyes, with which we view the physical world around us. In addition, the apostle Paul talks about a second set of eyes—the eyes of our heart that can be enlightened to perceive spiritual truth.

Paul said, "I pray that the eyes of your heart may be enlightened" (Eph. 1:18). This is my prayer for you. I am convinced that any believer can develop the seer capacity. All prophecy, including the seer dimension, is a sovereign gift of God, but I do not believe it is an exclusive gift. As you pray over the eyes of your heart, God will give you the spirit of wisdom and revelation in the knowledge of Him. You will come to know the Lord in a way you never could on your own or in your own wisdom.

As you go through this study guide, welcome the Holy Spirit to move your heart and stir up your hunger for intimacy with God. May the prophetic power of visions, dreams, and open heavens increase in your life so that you can accomplish the seer's ultimate goal: to reveal Christ Jesus.

With a passion for maturity in the Body of Christ,
James W. Goll

SECTION ONE

UNDERSTANDING THE SEER REALM

LESSON ONE

SEER AND PROPHET: TWO PROPHETIC STREAMS

I. **Defining Our Terms**

A. **Three Hebrew Words**

1. *Nabiy'* (pronounced naw-bee') is translated "prophet." The word "prophet" (in various forms) is used over 300 times in the Old Testament and 100 times in the New Testament.

    a. Young — "The function of a *nabiy'* was to speak a message on behalf of a superior. In the case of Aaron, this superior was Moses, although ultimately, of course, it was God. As far as the prophets were concerned, the superior was God Himself. It was He with whom the word to be spoken originated. He placed that word in the mouth of the prophets, and they in turn declared it unto the people…we conclude then, that upon the basis of Old Testament usage, the *nabiy'* was a speaker who declared the word that God had given him."[1]

    b. Scriptures
        i.   Deuteronomy 18:18
        ii.   Exodus 7:1
        iii. Exodus 4:15-16
        iv.   Jeremiah 1:5,9

2. *Ro'eh* or *ra'ah* and *chozeh* (pronounced *khaw-zah*) are translated "seer."

a. Young — "The word *nabiy'* stresses the active work of the prophet, in speaking forth the message from God. The word *ra'ah* on the other hand, brings to the fore the experience by means of which the prophet was made to 'see' that message. One word lays the emphasis upon the prophet's relation to the people; the other upon his relation to God."[2]

b. Hengsteuberg — "These were not so much chronological historians as much as describers of pictures."[3]

c. Scriptures
   i. First Samuel 9:9 — Samuel
   ii. Second Chronicles 29:30 — Asaph
   iii. Second Samuel 24:11 — Gad
   iv. Second Samuel 7:2 — Nathan

3. General Conclusion

a. Prophecy is God communicating His will by word (sometimes by action) through chosen persons. It includes whatever God desires to say about past, present, and future. Some people have tended to confine prophecy to words about the future, but this is inaccurate. The prophet was, and is, a forthteller as well as a foreteller. ***Indeed, he speaks whatever God wants said!***

b. The "seer" is the receptive dimension, and the "prophet" is the communicative dimension.

c. Bill Hamon, founder of Christian International Ministries Network, made a statement about two prophetic streams in the 1940s–50s that have re-emerged a generation later. "Two streams of restoration came forth in 1947–48. One was the 'Latter Rain Movement', which restored the practice of…the laying on of hands…as well as extensive congregational prophesying…. They emphasized moving into the prophetic realm by faith, grace and gifting. The other restoration stream was what was termed 'The Healing and Deliverance Movement.' Their restorational emphasis was laying on of hands for healing, deliverance and world evangelism by preaching with signs and wonders. Both groups were of God and were valid ministries."[4]

B.   **Words Describing How the Prophetic Comes**[5]

1.   *Nataph* — This means "to let drop like rain." It comes upon us little by little and is accumulated in our buckets over a period of time.

2.   *Massa* — This is used to refer to the "hand of the Lord" that releases the "burden of the Lord." When God's hand comes upon us, it imparts something to us. When His hand lifts, His burden remains.

3.   *Nabiy'* — This word refers to the action of "flowing forth." It also carries with it the thought "to bubble forth like a fountain, to let drop, to lift up, to tumble forth, and to spring forth."

4.   *Propheteia* — This New Testament Greek word means "speaking forth the mind and the counsel of God." It simply means "to speak for another."

C.   **Levels and Terms of "Seeing"**

1.   Visual — Insights, revelations, warnings, and prophecies from the Spirit of God may come in supernatural visual dreams. Herein one sees God's revelation while his spirit simply observes and receives the message. One might even see the heavens opened, as Ezekiel did (see Ezek. 1:1), even though he's asleep. In an open heaven type of a vision, the higher ethers (celestial realms) are disclosed, and views, patterns, and heavenly sights of God become seeable.

2.   Actual — Supernatural actual dreams are those in which God's tangible presence is evident. To see the Lord in a dream is *visual*, but for the Lord to manifest Himself to you in a dream is *actual*.

II.   **Similarities and Differences of the Streams**

A.   **The Prophet — *Nabiy'***

1.   Often uses plurality of eldership or seasoned, gifted individuals (men and women) with the "laying on of hands" to minister.

2.   Will utilize giftings of tongues and interpretation of tongues.

3.   Is associated with spontaneous, fast flow with inspiration being the tone.

4.   Often "hears" and repeats as spoken to.

5.   Steps out to prophesy according to his portion of faith.

6.   The prophetic presbytery is a common approach.

B.   **The Seer — *Ro'eh (Ra'ah)***

1.   Tends to be more single in ministry versus the plurality of a team.

2.   Emphasizes visions and the revelatory gifts versus the audible, speaking gifts.

3.   Often operates at a slower pace due to describing pictures in their own words.

4.   Is dependent upon the angelic and the manifested presence of God.

5.   Often has limitations until they sense the anointing.

6.   Often gets information ahead of time and tells it later.

III.   **Conclusion**

A.   **A Word in a Dream**

In a clear dream, Paul Cain came to me and said: "The seer hears as much as he sees; it's just a different deep touch from the same dear Jesus."

B.   **The Manifold Purpose**

The purpose of both the prophet and the seer is to reveal the glorious wonders of Jesus Christ, God's purpose in a generation, eternity, Heaven and hell, and the Father's great presence.

C.   **Pray**

Pray for your eyes to be opened.

In Ephesians 1:17-19 (NIV), Paul says, *"I keep asking that the God of our Lord Jesus Christ, the glorious Father, may give you the Spirit of wisdom and revelation, so that you may know Him better. I pray also that the eyes of your heart may be enlightened in order that you may know the hope to which He has called you, the riches of His glorious inheritance in the saints, and His incomparably great power for us who believe."*

And in Second Kings 6:17, the prophet Elisha prays: *"O Lord…open his eyes that he* [Elisha's servant] *may see."*

REFLECTIVE QUESTIONS
LESSON ONE

(Answers to these questions can be found in the back of the study guide.)

FILL IN THE BLANK

1. The seer tends to be the _____ dimension and the prophet tends to be the _____ dimension of the prophetic.

2. The Hebrew word _____ refers to the impartation and resultant burden from the Lord.

3. The Hebrew word _____ is the accumulated revelation that comes little by little.

MULTIPLE CHOICE:
CHOOSE FROM THE LIST BELOW TO ANSWER THE NEXT TWO QUESTIONS

A. *Nabiy'*   B. *Ro'eh*   C. *Propheteia*   D. *Massa*

4. The function of a _____ prophet is to speak a message on behalf of God.

5. The function of a _____ prophet is to see and describe that word.

TRUE OR FALSE

6. The purpose of both the seer and the prophet is to reveal Jesus. _____

7. *Propheteia* means to bubble up and flow forth. _____

8. Samuel and Gad were known as seers. _____

SCRIPTURE MEMORIZATION

9. Write out and memorize Deuteronomy 18:18.

PERSONAL REFLECTION

10.   What was the primary point you learned from this lesson?

Notes

LESSON TWO

DIMENSIONS OF THE PROPHETIC ANOINTING

The prophetic spirit can be expressed in various ways. For the purpose of broadening our horizon of how this revelatory presence can be received and released, let's consider seven of these expressions.

I. **Dreams and Visions**

   A. **Purpose**

      1. Dreams and visions awaken people to God and to the realm of the Holy Spirit, ministry of angels, etc.

      2. They creatively illumine the truth of God's word and ways.

      3. They confirm direction God has given others.

      4. They are miraculous and elevate our faith level to believe in God for His personal and corporate purposes to be fulfilled.

   B. **Biblical Example**

   Zechariah in the Old Testament (see Zech. 4:1-6).

   C. **Contemporary Examples**

   Bob Jones, John Paul Jackson, John Sandford, Jill Austin, and many others are examples of this type of vessel today. These individuals could have a combination of power, prophecy, and personal ministry impact and impartation. They operate primarily out of a seer dimension.

(For more on this subject, see the study guides *Experiencing Dreams and Visions and Understanding Supernatural Encounters.*)

II.   **Proclamation of God's Corporate Purpose**

    A.   **Purpose**

        1.   Gives clarity to the overall direction and purpose of the Body of Christ.

        2.   Enables the Body to reach full maturity in Christ.

        3.   A person who has a "proclamation of God's corporate purpose" often operates in the gift of "steerings," like the sons of Issachar (see 1 Chron. 12:32), so they interpret for us the big picture of what the Holy Spirit is saying.

    B.   **Biblical Examples**

        1.   Throughout the New Testament, the apostle Paul wonderfully paints with the spirit of revelation the purposes of God for His glorious end-time Bride to come forth.

        2.   Luke, the writer of the Book of Acts, became a chronicler of the movement of the Holy Spirit.

    C.   **Contemporary Examples**

    These could be prophetic teachers or those who chronicle the works of the Spirit. Possible examples are Rick Joyner, Bob Mumford, or the late Jamie Buckingham. Many are emerging with this interpretive skill upon them in this hour.

III.   **Proclamation of God's Heart Standards for His People**

    A.   **Purpose**

        1.   Calls for holy thoughts, intentions, motives, conviction, and methods for individuals, churches, ministries, etc.

        2.   Ushers in the fruit of the Holy Spirit—the character of Christ—purity and holiness.

        3.   Releases standards for the family, fatherhood of God, etc.

    B.   **Biblical Examples**

        1.   Moses called for the golden calf to be ground to dust and brought forth the Ten Commandments.

2. Isaiah had an experience of coals of fire cleansing him from uncleanness and preparing him for the Lord.

3. John the Baptist preached the message of repentance as a forerunner, preparing the way for Jesus.

C. Contemporary Examples

These are the prophetic evangelists or revivalists, calling us to repentance and preaching on the character of God. Examples today could be the late Leonard Ravenhill, David Wilkerson, Steve Hill, and others.

IV. Proclamation of the Church's Social Responsibilities and Actions

A. Purpose

1. Insists that the Church cares for the widow, the orphan, the poor, the oppressed, the prisoner, etc.

2. Calls into being the Lord's justice into the unjust society.

3. Righteousness is the torch that these compassionate broken vessels carry.

B. Biblical Examples

1. Amos in the Old Testament (see Amos 5:21-24).

2. James in the New Testament declares: Show your faith by your works (see James 2:21-26).

C. Contemporary Examples

These people wed together the gifts of compassion, mercy, and the prophetic. They speak to society, as well as to the Church. Norm Stone with Walk Across America for Life, Beverly LaHaye with Concerned Women for America, Chuck Colson with Prison Fellowship, Marcus Young with Divine Inheritance and many others could be examples of this today.

V. Speaking Forth the Administrative Strategy of God With a Political Slant

A. Purpose

1. Wise and smooth implementation of God's purposes.

2. Provision released during difficult hours.

3. Moves into the Spirit of Counsel for those in authority.

B.   **Biblical Examples**

    1.   Joseph in the Old Testament brought into being a strategy of economic proportions, wedding together the revelatory and administrative giftings.

    2.   Agabus in the Book of Acts declared a famine was coming and called for the necessary plans of provisions to be made.

C.   **Contemporary Examples**

These individual men and women combine administration, history of the church, and various cultures with a prophetic expression. There is possibly a mix of the prophetic and the apostolic in these people. Dennis Peacocke, Lance Wallneau and Beth Alves with Increase International are a few of today's examples.

VI.   **Prophetic Worship Leaders Who Usher in the Manifested Presence of God Through Prophetic Worship**

A.   **Purpose**

    1.   Releases people into liberty to both express and receive God's love.

    2.   The gifts of the Holy Spirit are easily received and released in such an atmosphere.

    3.   Spiritual warfare often takes place as "high praise" defeating the works of the enemy.

B.   **Biblical Examples**

    1.   David played his harp and demons departed from Saul (see 1 Sam. 18:10).

    2.   Miriam changed the desert into a dancing floor (see Exod. 15:20).

    3.   Deborah and Barak sang forth the "prophetic word" (see Judg. 5:1-31).

C.   **Contemporary Examples**

David Ruis, Kent Henry, Brian Doerksen, Robert Stearns, JoAnn McFatter, Julie Meyer, Jason Upton and many others.

VII.   **Prophetic Intercession**

A.   **Purpose**

    1.   Receives the burden of God and releases intercession, which can affect international affairs (particularly political burdens).

2.   Kneels on the revealed promises and prays the prophetic into being.

3.   These are often "crisis intercessors" who are landed on by the Holy Spirit for individual or corporate emergency situations.

B.   Biblical Examples

1.   Daniel prayed three times a day for God's sovereign purpose with Israel and her release from Babylonian captivity.

2.   Anna is a New Testament model who prepared the way for the Messiah to come through her ministry of prayer and fasting (see Luke 2:36-38).

3.   Esther declared a fast in a time of crisis, saving her people from annihilation (see Esther 4:14-16).

C.   Contemporary Examples

Cindy Jacobs, Tom Hess, Lou Engle, Dick Simmons, Jean Krisle Blasie, Rick Ridings, and a host of revelatory gifted intercessors are examples.

(For more on this subject, see the study guide *Compassionate Prophetic Intercession* and the book *The Prophetic Intercessor*.)

VIII.   Varieties of Prophetic Anointings

A.   The Kingdom Versus the Church

1.   Some are placed in the church for ministry to the church. Others are placed in the church for ministry to the secular community.

2.   With government or without? Some prophetic vessels carry governmental leadership anointing (Moses, Abraham, David, etc.). Others do not and should not. Let us not covet another person's grace allotment.

B.   Other Possible Categories Needed Today

These are simply a few additional examples of the variety of prophetic anointings the Holy Spirit wants to release.

1.   Spirit-Bearers

        a.   John 3:8 says: *"The wind blows where it wishes, and you hear the sound of it, but cannot tell where it comes from and where it goes. So is everyone who is born of the Spirit"* (NKJV).

b. Spirit-bearers practice the presence of Jesus, releasing the ordinary manifestations of God's glorious presence, through a love-walk.

c. These people can experience extraordinary manifestations, such as falling in the Spirit, quaking, shaking, ecstatic speech, power encounters, kingdom clashes of angelic and demonic warfare, angelic activity, fragrance of Christ, etc.

2. Prophetic Counselors

This is a combination of the pastoral and prophetic. Often mingled with the spirit of counsel and understanding (gifts of healings and discerning of spirits). Their concern is with the internal condition of the heart and mind of man.

3. Prophetic Equippers

This is a prophetic and teacher combination. They explain the ways of the Spirit, taking the bizarre and making it practical, relatable, and understandable. Their call is to multiply and disciple.

4. Prophetic Writers

This is a gift-mix of writing and prophetic. They write with revelatory anointing, expressing God's heart to contemporary society. Examples today are John Bibee (children's literature) and Francis Schaeffer.

5. Prophetic Evangelist

This is taking the revelatory gifts to the streets, stadiums, neighborhoods, health clubs, executive places, etc. This is one of the primary corners we need to turn in our day. We need a company of Prophetic Evangelists to arise!

This is not an exhaustive list by any means! This simply gives us a broader look at the prophetic and how desperately we need it in every area of culture and life. We must bring God's Kingdom to bear in every arena and these are but a few of the needed expressions to bring greater impact for such a time as this for Jesus Christ's sake.

REFLECTIVE QUESTIONS
LESSON TWO

(Answers to these questions can be found in the back of the study guide.)

FILL IN THE BLANK

1.   Name at least three ways the prophetic is expressed. _____
_____ _____.

2.   Amos 5:24: "But let justice roll on like a river, _____ like a never failing stream!"

3.   The Hebrew word *chozeh* means _____.

MULTIPLE CHOICE: CHOOSE FROM THE LIST BELOW TO ANSWER THE NEXT TWO QUESTIONS

A. Dreams and visions   B. Prophetic worship   C. Prophetic intercession   D. Heart standards

4.   _____ receives the burden of God and releases intercession.

5.   God's _____ usher in the purity and holiness of Jesus.

TRUE OR FALSE

6.   Proclamation of God's corporate purpose gives overall direction to the Body of Christ. _____

7.   Seers primarily operate out of dreams and visions. _____

8.   Proclamation of social responsibilities is for the purpose of intercession. _____

SCRIPTURE MEMORIZATION

9.   Write out and memorize Luke 2:36-38.

PERSONAL REFLECTION

10.   What was the primary point you learned from this lesson?

Notes

LESSON THREE

VISION: THE POWER
THAT SUSTAINS

I. **Scriptural Review on Being a People of Vision**

Read the following Scriptures and the brief explanation that follows.

A. **Primary Verse — Proverbs 29:18**

"Where there is no vision [revelation] *the people are unrestrained* [perish]*"* (Prov. 29:18). We must learn to set a goal or target in front of our eyes to gaze upon. When you aim at something, you will surely hit it! Therefore, let us set our sights and aim at God's goals (see Phil. 3:13-15).

B. **Second Kings 6:14-17**

Elisha saw the host of God encompassing the city of Dothan and was therefore strengthened in God. He knew there were more with us than those with the enemy (in the world).

C. **Zechariah 4:1-7**

Zechariah was roused by an angel and was asked what he saw. He gave the right, humble, true answer. He realized the Lord also had the interpretation of the revelation and asked, "What is this?" God response was, "[It's] not by might, nor by power, but by My Spirit" (Zech. 4:6).

D. **Daniel 7:1-13**

This shows the progression of how Daniel worked with revelation. He recorded a summary of it and kept looking for a revelation of the Lord

Himself. Let's learn the lesson and do the same. It is by keeping our vision of Him clear that we are sustained in our many labors of life and ministry.

E.   **Ephesians 1:17-19**

Continue to pray this verse over your life. Ask the Holy Spirit on an ongoing basis to give you the spirit of wisdom and revelation in the knowledge of the Lord Jesus Christ. Ask that the eyes of your heart (faith, understanding) be opened like the shutter lens of a camera. Let more "light" come in and God's picture (vision) be developed inside. Also pray for a revelation of the greatness of God's power toward us who believe and the glorious inheritance in the saints.

F.   **Acts 7:55-56**

As Stephen was stoned, being full of the Holy Spirit, he gazed intently into Heaven and saw the glory of God, and Jesus standing at the right hand of God; and he said, *"Behold, I see the heavens opened up and the Son of Man standing at the right hand of God."*

Once again, let's keep the lens of our camera focused in the right direction. Let's keep looking at Christ Jesus the Lord!

G.   **Acts 26:16-20**

Paul stands before King Agrippa and proclaims, *"I did not prove to be disobedient to the heavenly vision."* Let this be our goal as well. Let's be apprehended by a heavenly vision!

II.   **Developing Our Capacity to See in the Holy Spirit**

A.   **Quotes From Christian Leaders**

1.   Dr. David Yonggi Cho — "The language of the Holy Spirit is dreams and visions." As Dr. Cho teaches, we must learn to look past the temporal into the eternal—into the fourth dimension.

2.   Watchman Nee — "The picture is the Holy Spirit's memory."

B.   **Jesus Our Model**

1.   John 5:19-20

"Jesus gave them this answer: 'I tell you the truth, the Son can do nothing by Himself; He can do only what He sees His Father doing, because whatever the Father does the Son also does. For the Father loves the Son and shows Him all

He does. Yes, to your amazement He will show Him even greater things than these'" (NIV). Jesus did nothing of Himself. He only did those things which He saw the Father doing. This is our model and example. Let us "look to see" what our Father is initiating and respond to His activity.

2. John 8:38

    "I speak the things which I have seen with My Father; therefore you also do the things which you heard from your Father." We each respond to the authorities that govern us. Let's look to our Father and do what He is doing.

C. **Lessons From the Life of Jacob**

To properly understand the following section, it will be necessary to read each of the Scripture passages listed.

1. Genesis 30:31-36

    Jacob and Laban divide the flocks. Jacob takes all the speckled, spotted, and black lambs. Laban is left with the pure ones.

2. Genesis 30:37,39

    Jacob took fresh rods of almond (tree symbolizes authority) and peeled white stripes in them. He placed them at the watering troughs where the flocks came to drink. The flocks then brought forth striped, speckled, and spotted offspring.

3. Genesis 30:40-43

    Jacob prospers exceedingly as the strong sheep produce the desired result. The principle is: vision is the power that sustains. What you keep in front of your eyes will determine your outcome.

4. Genesis 31:1-13

    Jacob is now vindicated. God shows him in a dream that this is His way of restoring Jacob's fortune.

III. **The Principle of Presentation**

A. **Romans 6:13**

    "Present yourselves to God as those alive from the dead and your members as instruments of righteousness to God." To whom we present our "members"

(individual parts) they become a slave. If we present them to righteousness, then they become a slave to righteousness; if to sin then they become a slave to sin.

B. **Ephesians 1:17-19**

With this principle in mind, let us present our members (individual parts) to the Lord to be His slaves. Let us now present our "eyes" to be His slaves. The eye is the window of the soul. Remember, what we keep in front of our eyes, we become. Let us now present our eyes (mind, heart, etc.) and ask for the spirit of revelation to be granted.

C. **Second Kings 6:17**

Similar to Elisha, we should pray, *"O Lord, open the eyes of Your servants that they might see."*

Take these verses and others and regularly ask the Lord to do what only He can. Ask Him to give you the *vision: for it is the power that sustains!*

REFLECTIVE QUESTIONS
LESSON THREE

(Answers to these questions can be found in the back of the study guide.)

FILL IN THE BLANK

1. Second Kings 6:17: "And Elisha _____, 'O Lord, _____ his eyes so he may see'…and he looked and saw the hills full of horses and chariots of fire all around Elisha."

2. John 8:38: "I speak the things which I _____ with My Father [in My Father's presence]; therefore you also do the things which you heard from your father."

3. John 5:19: "The Son can do nothing by Himself; He can do only what He sees His _____ doing, because whatever the _____ does the Son also does" (NIV).

MULTIPLE CHOICE: CHOOSE FROM THE LIST BELOW TO ANSWER THE NEXT TWO QUESTIONS

A. Revelation   B. Light   C. Dream   D. Vision

4. Acts 26:19 says, "I did not prove to be disobedient to the heavenly _____."

5. Lord, let more _____ come in and God's picture (vision) be developed inside.

TRUE OR FALSE

6. What you keep in front of your eyes will determine your outcome. _____

7. Where there is no vision the people perish. _____

8. The language of the Holy Spirit is dreams and visions. _____

SCRIPTURE MEMORIZATION

9.   Write out and memorize Proverbs 29:18 and Ephesians 1:17-19 (or another Scripture from Section One).

PERSONAL REFLECTION

10.   What was the primary point you learned from this lesson?

Notes

LESSON FOUR

THE DIVERSITY OF VISIONARY STATES

There is only one Holy Spirit, but He works in many different ways. There are many spiritual gifts, but only one gift giver: the Holy Spirit of God. The prophetic anointing manifests itself in many diverse ways, but they all derive from the same Spirit. This same diversity by the one Spirit also applies to visionary states and experience. Let's take a closer look at some of these visionary states.

I.   **Greek Words for Visionary States**

The following are eight Greek words that describe a different aspect of visionary revelation.

A.   *Onar*

The common word for "dream." Everyday dreams are visionary in nature because our minds generate images that we "see" while we are asleep.

1.   Joseph, Jesus' earthly father (see Matt. 1:20; 2:13, 19-21).

2.   The wise men (see Matt. 2:12).

3.   Pontius Pilate (see Matt. 27:19).

B.   *Enupnion (Enupniazomai)*

A vision received while asleep. It stresses the sudden, shocking quality of the content contained in that dream.

1.   Acts 2:17

"'And it shall be in the last days,' God says, 'that I will pour forth of My spirit on all mankind; and your sons and your daughters shall prophesy, and your young men shall see visions, and your old men shall dream [enupnion] *dreams* [enupniazomai].'"*

2. Jude 8-9

Yet in the same way these men, also by dreaming [enupniazomai], *defile the flesh, and reject authority, and revile angelic majesties. But Michael the archangel, when he disputed with the devil and argued about the body of Moses, did not dare pronounce against him a railing judgment, but said, "The Lord rebuke you!"*

C. *Horama*

This word is translated "vision" and can refer to visions of the night or sleeping experiences, as well as to waking visions. New Testament examples commonly associate this word with *waking visions.*

1. Peter, James, and John at the transfiguration of Jesus (see Matt. 17:9)

2. God's instructions to Ananias to go to Saul (see Acts 9:10-12)

3. Cornelius's visitation by an angel (see Acts 10:3-4)

4. Peter ponders the meaning of his vision before the men sent by Cornelius arrive (see Acts 10:19-20).

5. Paul's vision of a man from Macedonia (see Acts 16:9-10)

6. Paul's vision to settle and preach in Corinth (see Acts 18:9-11)

D. *Horasis*

This word only occurs three times in the Greek New Testament. It refers to sight or vision in either an external or internal sense. The Greek language makes no distinction between the perception of the physical eye and the non-physical eye. Both the natural and the spiritual are considered general perception.

In Ephesians 1:18, the apostle Paul was referring to the "eyes" of our heart with which we see into the spiritual realm: *"I pray that the eyes of your heart may be enlightened...."* Simply stated, a vision—a *horasis*—occurs when the Spirit who lives within us looks out through the "windows" of our eyes and allows us to see what He sees.

1. Acts 2:17 says, *"Your young men shall see visions* [horasis]*."*

2. Revelation 4:3 (KJV) says, *"And He that sat was to look upon* [horasis] *like a jasper and a sardine stone: and there was a rainbow round about the throne, in sight like unto an emerald."*

3. Revelation 9:17 says, *"And thus I saw the horses in the vision* [horasis]*...."*

E. *Optasia*

It is translated "visuality," or in concrete form, "apparition." It has the sense of self-disclosure or of letting oneself be seen. The word occurs four times in the New Testament and always in the context of someone seeing a divine or spiritual personage.

1. Zechariah sees a vision of Gabriel announcing the birth of his son, John the Baptist (see Luke 1:22).

2. Two of Jesus' disciples on the road to Emmaus describe the vision the women saw of angels who said that Jesus was alive (see Luke 24:22-23).

3. Paul uses this word to describe visions the Lord has given to him (see 2 Cor. 12:1-4).

4. Acts 26:19 (KJV) says, *"I was not disobedient unto the heavenly vision* [optasia]*...."*

F. *Ekstasis*

We derive the English word "ecstasy" from this word. It literally means "standing aside from oneself, being displaced or over against oneself," and ordinarily there is a sense of amazement, bewilderment, confusion, and even extreme terror.

1. It is the response of the crowd who witnessed Jesus' healing of a paralyzed man whose friends had lowered him through the roof in order to get him to Jesus (see Luke 5:26).

2. We also see it in the women's response to the angelic visitation at the empty tomb (see Mark 16:8).

3. It is the amazement of the people who saw the beggar born lame walking and praising God (see Acts 3:9-10).

4. *Ekstasis* also means "trance," as in Acts 10:10 when Peter has his vision on a rooftop before his visit from Cornelius.

5. Paul fell into a trance while praying in the temple and saw the Lord telling him to get out of Jerusalem quickly (see Acts 22:17).

G. *Apokalupsis*

Translated "revelation," it literally means disclosure, divine uncovering, or revelation. It carries specifically the sense of something hidden that has now been uncovered or revealed. For many people, the Book of Revelation is full of puzzles and mysteries. It is important to remember that "apocalypse," or *apokalupsis*, does not mean "hidden," but "revelation," or an "unveiling." We can expect the Holy Spirit to reveal mysteries to us through the Word of God and supernatural encounters of a heavenly kind!

1.   Romans 16:25-27

"Now to Him who is able to establish you according to my gospel and the preaching of Jesus Christ, according to the revelation [apokalupsis] of the mystery which has been kept secret for long ages past, but now is manifested, and by the Scriptures of the prophets, according to the commandment of the eternal God, has been made known to all the nations, leading to obedience of faith; to the only wise God, through Jesus Christ, be the glory forever. Amen."

2.   Ephesians 1:17

"That the God of our Lord Jesus Christ, the Father of glory, may give to you a spirit of wisdom and of revelation [apokalupsis] in the knowledge of Him."

3.   First Peter 1:6-7,13

Apokalupsis also appears in connection with the revelation or appearing of Christ.

"In this you greatly rejoice, even though now for a little while, if necessary, you have been distressed by various trials, so that the proof of your faith, being more precious that gold which is perishable, even though tested by fire, may be found to result in praise and glory and honor at the revelation [apokalupsis] of Jesus Christ...Therefore, prepare your minds for action, keep sober in spirit, fix your hope completely on the grace to be brought to you at the revelation [apokalupsis] of Jesus Christ."

4.   Also see First Corinthians 14:6,26; Second Corinthians 12:1,7; and Galatians 2:2.

H. *Egenomhn en pneumati*

This phrase is translated "to become in Spirit." This refers to the state in which one could see visions and be informed or spoken to directly by the

Spirit. We must remember that we receive insight by first getting in the Spirit. The more we are filled with the Spirit and walk in the Spirit, the more we become one with the Spirit, and the more our eyes will be opened to see in the Spirit. He will give us the perception to look into the spiritual realm.

John, the writer of Revelation, may have been in a trance state—*ekstasis*—during the time he received his revelation from the Lord. Although John does not use that word to describe his state, he does use the phrase *egenomhn en pneumati*, which means "I was in the Spirit."

1.   Revelation 1:9-10

"I, John, your brother and fellow partaker in the tribulation and kingdom and perseverance which are in Jesus, was on the island called Patmos because of the word of the God and the testimony of Jesus. I was in the Spirit [egenomhn en pneumati] *on the Lord's day, and I heard behind me a loud voice like the sound of a trumpet."*

2.   Also see Matthew 4:1; Mark 1:12; Luke 1:41; and Luke 4:1-2.

II.   Closing

Let us each pray that the eyes of our heart will be enlightened that we might see. As mentioned earlier, in Lesson Three, Dr. David Yonggi Cho stated, "The language of the Holy Spirit is dreams and visions." Watchman Nee said, "The picture is the Holy Spirit's memory." Let us learn to use the natural and supernatural tools the Lord has given us and see what God is doing.

REFLECTIVE QUESTIONS
LESSON FOUR

(Answers to these questions can be found in the back of the study guide.)

FILL IN THE BLANK

1.   There are many _____ _____, but only one _____ _____.

2.   The language of the Holy Spirit is _____ and _____.

3.   According to Watchman Nee, the _____ is the Holy Spirit's memory.

MULTIPLE CHOICE: CHOOSE FROM THE LIST BELOW TO ANSWER THE NEXT TWO QUESTIONS

A. Visions   B. End times   C. Dreams   D. Revelation

4.   Everyday _____ are visionary in nature because our minds generate images that we "see" while we are asleep.

5.   "Apocalypse," or *apokalupsis*, does not mean "hidden," but "_____."

TRUE OR FALSE

6.   The more we are filled with the Spirit and walk in the Spirit, the more we become one with the Spirit, and the more our eyes will be opened to see in the Spirit. _____

7.   There is little evidence that the followers of Christ received visionary revelation. _____

8.   We need to learn to use the supernatural tools the Lord has given us. _____

SCRIPTURE MEMORIZATION

9.   Write out and memorize Romans 16:25-27.

Personal Reflection

10.   What was the primary point you learned from this lesson?

Notes

Section Two

Spiritual Discernment

LESSON FIVE

WISELY JUDGING REVELATORY ENCOUNTERS

I. Introduction

God still speaks today through many different avenues: channels of visions, dreams, inner knowings, the audible and inner voice, journaling, creation, and most importantly, through the *logos,* canon of Scripture. The interpretation of revelation makes it imperative that we pray for the spirit of wisdom, understanding, and the counsel of the Lord. In this lesson, we will probe into the necessary subject of "Wisely Judging Revelatory Encounters."

It is absolutely imperative that you know and study the Bible so you have an absolute standard against which to test all spiritual experiences. The Bible is our absolute, infallible, unchanging standard of truth. Just as you learn to crawl before you learn to walk, so too, before you learn to work with *rhema* (the revealed "now" word of God), you should know the *logos* (the written word of God). You should, at least, have a working knowledge of the New Testament and be working on the rest of the Bible if you are going to investigate *rhema* revelation in depth. Otherwise, you open yourself up to easy deception.

God has also given us each other, and together, we are the Body of Christ. We find safety in our relationship to a Bible-believing fellowship. Ephesians 5:21 (KJV) states, *"[Sub-mit] yourselves one to another,"* and goes on to delineate the various areas of covering God has placed in our lives. *"In the multitude of counselors there is safety"* (Prov. 11:14 NKJV). In an age of lawlessness, we must be under the umbrella covering of the Lord, His Word, and the local church to protect us from the spirit of the world. Let us not be proud individuals "doing our thing," but let us be humble servants committed to a local expression of Christ's Body, diligently studying the Scriptures, daily in prayer, and led by the Spirit of Truth into His purposes and individual will for our lives.

Two foundational questions should first be answered positively in our search to discern God's voice:

> A.   Are you regularly studying the Scriptures and maintaining a life of prayer?
>
> B.   Are you a functional member of a local Christian congregation?

Let us lay these two building blocks firmly in place as we investigate the principles of testing spiritual experiences.

My prayer is that this lesson on "Wisely Judging Revelatory Encounters" will add godly wisdom and discernment to our lives. Remember to *"examine everything carefully; hold fast to that which is good"* (1 Thess. 5:21).

II.   Sources of Revelation

The Scriptures teach us that revelation can possibly come from any one of these three sources:

A.   The Holy Spirit

The Holy Spirit is the only true source of revelation. Read Second Peter 1:21. The Holy Spirit "moved" these prophets. The Greek word for "moved" is *phero*, which means "to be borne along" or even "to be driven along as a wind."[6] Read also Acts 27:15-17.

B.   The Human Spirit

Read Ezekiel 13:1-6 and Jeremiah 23:16. This is one who is speaking out of his own heart. His revelation is not born from God, but is out of his own imaginations of his spirit or soul. Ezekiel 13:1-2 says, *"That prophesy, out of their own hearts... Woe unto the foolish prophets that follow their own spirit and have seen nothing."*

C.   The Evil Spirit

The source of this instance is satanic as a lying spirit. Consider Acts 16:16-18 about the slave girl with the spirit of divination. She spoke truth, but it was from a wrong source. Paul addresses the spirit of divination and commands it to leave her.

III.   Dealing With Mixture

Revelation can even be a mixture of any of these sources. This is possible because men, as prophetic mouthpieces, are yet in an imperfect state. No prophetic ministry, except that of Christ, was ever a perfect channel.

A.   Life of Peter

Read Matthew 16:16-22. One moment Peter gives a strong, current, revelatory word; minutes later he states that Jesus should never die, go to the cross, etc. Jesus recognized the latter as satan and He rebuked satan as he spoke through Peter's lips (see Matt. 16:23). Read also First Thessalonians 5:20.

B.   Things Affecting Your Spirit

For the Christian, God's Spirit is in union with your spirit (see 1 Cor. 6:17); however, things other than God can affect and move your spirit and soul.

1.   Circumstances of life (see 1 Sam. 1:1-15)

2.   Physical, bodily circumstances (see 1 Sam. 30:12)

3.   Satan (see John 13:2)

4.   Man's undisciplined life (see Prov. 16:32)

C.   Questions to Ask

As your mind goes to the work of purifying and *rhema*, it should:

1.   Look for evidence of influences other than the Spirit of God.

2.   Ask, "What is the essence of the Word?"

3.   Discern whether you were under the control of the Holy Spirit as you received your revelation by asking these questions:

a.   Have you presented your life as a living sacrifice?

b.   Have you been obedient to His Word?

c.   Are you being enlightened with His inspiration?

d.   Are you committed to doing His will?

e.   Are you yielding your life to praise...or critical speech?

f.   Are you waiting quietly and expectantly before Him?

D. Test Whether an Image Is From Self, satan, or God[7]

    1.   I am to instantly cut off all pictures put before my mind's eye by satan (see Matt. 5:28; 2 Cor. 10:5).

    2.   I am to present the eyes of my heart to the Lord for Him to fill. In this way, I prepare myself to receive (see Rev. 4:1).

    3.   The Spirit is to project on my inner screen the flow of vision that He desires (see Rev. 4:2).

IV. Nine Scriptural Tests[8]

A. First Corinthians 14:3

"But one who prophesies speaks to men for edification and exhortation and consolation."

The end purpose of all true prophetical revelation is to build up, to admonish, and to encourage the people of God. Anything that is not directed to this end is not true prophecy. Consider Jeremiah 1:5-10. His commission is at first negative, but then with a promise. First Corinthians 14:26 sums it up best: *"Let all things be done for edification."*

B. Second Timothy 3:16

"All Scripture is given by inspiration of God" (NKJV).

All true revelation always agrees with the letter and the spirit of Scripture. Read Second Corinthians 1:17-20. Where the Holy Spirit says yea and amen in Scripture, He also says yea and amen in revelation. He does not contradict Himself.

C. John 16:14

"He will glorify Me, for He will take of Mine and will disclose it to you."

All true revelation centers in Jesus Christ, and exalts and glorifies Him. Read Revelation 19:10.

D. Matthew 7:15-16

"Beware of false prophets, who come to you in sheep's clothing, but inwardly they are ravenous wolves. You will know them by their fruits" (NKJV).

True revelation produces fruit in character and conduct that agrees with the fruit of the Holy Spirit. Read Ephesians 5:9 and Galatians 5:22-23. Among aspects of character or conduct that are clearly not the fruit of the Holy Spirit, we may mention the following: pride, arrogance, boastfulness, exaggeration, dishonesty, covetousness, financial irresponsibility, licentiousness, immorality, addictive appetites, broken marriage vows, and broken homes. Any revelation that is responsible for results such as these is from a channel other than the Holy Spirit.

E.   Deuteronomy 18:20-22

" 'But the prophet who speaks a word presumptuously in My name which I have not commanded him to speak, or which he speaks in the name of other gods, that prophet shall die.' You may say in your heart, 'How will we know the word which the Lord has not spoken?' When a prophet speaks in the name of the Lord, if the thing does not come about or come true, that is the thing which the Lord has not spoken. The prophet has spoken it presumptuously; you shall not be afraid of him."

If a revelation contains prediction concerning the future, are these predictions fulfilled? If not, with a few exceptions, the revelation is not from God. Exceptions include:

1.   The will of the person involved.

2.   National repentance (e.g. Nineveh).

3.   Messianic predictions (hundreds of years until fulfilled).

4.   Note difference between Old and New Testament prophets.

F.   Deuteronomy 13:1-5

"If a prophet or a dreamer of dreams arises among you and gives you a sign or a wonder, and the sign or the wonder comes true, concerning which he spoke to you, saying, 'Let us go after other gods (whom you have not known) and let us serve them,' you shall not listen to the words of that prophet or that dreamer of dreams; for the Lord your God is testing you to find out if you love the Lord your God with all your heart and with all your soul. You shall follow the Lord your God and fear Him; and you shall keep His commandments, listen to His voice, serve Him, and cling to Him. But that prophet or that dreamer of dreams shall be put to death, because he has counseled rebellion against the Lord your God who brought you from the land of Egypt and redeemed you from the house of

slavery, to seduce you from the way in which the Lord your God commanded you to walk."

The fact that a person makes a prediction concerning the future that is fulfilled does not necessarily prove that that person is moving by Holy Spirit-inspired revelation. If such a person, by his own ministry, turns others away from obedience to the one true God, then that person is false—even if he makes correct predictions concerning the future.

G.   **Romans 8:15**

"For you have not received a spirit of slavery leading to fear again, but you have received a spirit of adoption as sons by which we cry out, 'Abba, Father!'"

True revelation, given by the Holy Spirit, produces liberty and not bondage. Read also First Corinthians 14:33 and Second Timothy 1:7. The Holy Spirit never brings God's people into a condition where they act like slaves, motivated by fear and legal compulsion.

H.   **Second Corinthians 3:6**

"Who also made us adequate as servants of a new covenant, not of the letter, but of the Spirit; for the letter kills, but the Spirit gives life."

True revelation, given by the Holy Spirit, produces life and not death.

I.   **First John 2:27**

"And as for you, the anointing which you received from Him abides in you, and you have no need for anyone to teach you; but as His anointing teaches you about all things, and is true and is not a lie, and just as it has taught you, you abide in Him."

True revelation, given by the Holy Spirit, is attested by the Holy Spirit within the believer. The Holy Spirit is "the Spirit of Truth" (John 16:13). He bears witness to that which is true, but He rejects that which is false. This ninth test is the *most subjective* of them all and must be used in conjunction with the previous eight objective standards.

V.   **Test Every Spirit to See if It Be of God**

A.   **First John 4:1-3**

"Dear friends, do not believe every spirit, but test the spirits to see whether they are from God, because many false prophets have gone out into the world. This is how you

can recognize the Spirit of God: Every spirit that acknowledges that Jesus Christ has come in the flesh is from God, but every spirit that does not acknowledge Jesus is not from God. This is the spirit of the antichrist, which you have heard is coming and even now is already in the world" (NIV).

B. Prophecy Is *Not* Perfect in Its Delivery

Inscripturated revelation was perfect and inerrant; however, revelation does not function on this sphere of inspiration. Thus, there is always the possibility of mixture in the revelatory word. Read First Corinthians 14:29. The fact that prophecy is open for judgment in this age proves its present, imperfect state. The imperfect state of prophecy is because of the imperfect state of the channel of man through which it comes.

C. Conclusion: Proving Revelation

1. Judge the content by:

    a. The principles of the written Word.

    b. Comparing revelation to the written Word.

    c. The commandments of the written Word.

2. First Thessalonians 5:20-21 says: *"Do not despise prophetic utterances, but examine everything carefully; hold fast to that which is good."*

VI. The Need for the Gift of Discerning of Spirits

Because the outward appearance of the wolf is disguised under "sheep's clothing," the human eye does not immediately discern the true identity of the wolf. However, there is one animal normally connected with the protection of sheep that will not be deceived by the "sheep's clothing." That animal is the sheep dog. He is not deceived because he does not judge by his eyesight, but by his sense of smell. ***The wolf may look like a sheep, but he still smells like a wolf.***

In Scripture, this sense of smell, acting independently of the eyesight, sometimes typifies the discernment that comes through the Holy Spirit. In Isaiah 11:2-3, the prophet, foreseeing the ministry of Jesus as the Messiah (the Anointed One), declares that *"the Spirit of the Lord…shall make him of quick understanding* [literally, quick of scent] *in the fear of the Lord: and He shall not judge after the sight of His eyes, neither reprove after the hearing of His ears."*

Those to whom God commits the care of His sheep must likewise, through the Holy Spirit, be "quick of scent," so that *they will not judge after the sight of their eyes, neither reprove after the hearing of their ears.* In this way, they will not depend merely on the evidence of their senses or the reasoning of their natural mind, but will quickly detect the false prophets who come among God's people as "wolves in sheep's clothing."

The sheep dog that fails to bark when the wolf approaches has failed in his responsibility to the flock. In Isaiah 56:10, God says concerning Israel's watchmen under the old covenant, *"They are all dumb dogs, they cannot bark; sleeping, lying down, loving to slumber."* These watchmen of Israel failed God and their people. When the spiritual enemies of God's people approached, these men remained silent and gave no warning to the flock. As a result, God's people became an easy prey to their enemies. The same thing has happened many times to God's people, even in this generation.

REFLECTIVE QUESTIONS
LESSON FIVE

(Answers to these questions can be found in the back of the study guide.)

FILL IN THE BLANK

1. Second Peter 1:20 says, "For _____ never had its origin in the will of man, but men spoke from God as they were _____ along by the Holy Spirit."

2. The Greek word *phero* means "moved or carried" and gives the idea to _____
    _____
    _____.

3. Sources of revelation can be the _____ Spirit, the
    _____ _____, or an _____
    _____.

MULTIPLE CHOICE: CHOOSE FROM THE LIST BELOW TO ANSWER THE NEXT TWO QUESTIONS

A. Glorify   B. Magnify   C. Love   D. Slavery

4. John 16:14 says, "He will _____ Me; for He will take of Mine, and will disclose it to you."

5. Romans 8:15 says, "For you have not received a spirit of _____ leading to fear again."

TRUE OR FALSE

6. True revelation given by the Holy Spirit is attested by the Holy Spirit within the believer. _____

7.   Because of mixture in one's spirit, it is possible to give an accurate prophetic word, but then speak as you are moved through by satan. _____

8.   A person who predicts accurately the future means they are flowing in the Holy Spirit. _____

SCRIPTURE MEMORIZATION

9.   Write out and memorize Second Peter 1:21 and First John 2:27.

PERSONAL REFLECTION

10.   What was the primary point you learned from this lesson?

Notes

DISCERNING OF SPIRITS

I. **The Discerning of Spirits Defined**

A. **Kenneth Hagin—Father of the Word of Faith Movement**

The discerning of spirits gives insight into the spirit world. It has to do with spirits, both good and bad. It is supernatural insight into the realm of spirits. To discern means to see—whether it be divine spirits, evil spirits, the human spirit, or even the discerning of the similitude of God.[9]

B. **Dick Iverson—Former Senior Pastor, Portland Bible Temple**

The gift of discerning spirits is the God-given ability or enablement to recognize the identity (and very often personality and condition) of the spirits which are behind different manifestations or activities. To "discern" means to perceive, distinguish, or differentiate. The dividing line between human and divine operation may be obscure to some believers, but one with the faculty of spiritual discernment sees a clear separation.[10]

C. **Derek Prince—Author and International Bible Teacher**

Discerning of spirits is the supernatural ability to recognize and distinguish between not only good and bad, but various classes of spirits:

1. The Holy Spirit

2. Good angels

3. Fallen angels

4. Demons or evil spirits

5. The human spirit.

"Discernment" is a form of direct perception where "knowledge" is the impartation of fact.[11]

D. David Pytches—Former Anglican Bishop, Author

This is a supernatural gift of perception given sovereignly by God to enable individuals in the church to distinguish the motivating spirit behind certain words or deeds.[12]

E. John Wimber—The Late Vineyard Ministries International Leader

Discerning of spirits is the supernatural capacity to judge whether the spirit operating has a source that is human, demonic, or divine. It is a supernatural perception in the spiritual realm for the purpose of determining the source of spiritual activity.[13]

F. Francis Frangipane—Author, Noted Speaker on Spiritual Warfare

Spiritual discernment is the grace to see into the unseen. It is a gift *of the Spirit* to perceive what is *in the spirit.* Its purpose is to see into the nature of that which is veiled[14] (see 1 Cor. 12:10; Acts 5:1-11; 16:16-18; 1 John 4:1-6; Matt. 16:21-23).

II. Examples of Discerning of Spirits

The following is a brief scriptural example of the four categories of discerning of spirits.

A. Discerning of the Holy Spirit

1. John 1:32-33 — John the Baptist discerns the Holy Spirit upon Jesus like a dove as He descended from Heaven.

2. Acts 2:3 — The believers in the upper room discern the Holy Spirit as the sound of rushing wind and then as tongues of fire resting on their heads.

B. Discerning of Angels

1. Luke 22:43 — An angel appears to Jesus in the garden of Gethsemane.

2. John 20:11-13 — Mary sees two angels in the sepulcher where Jesus had been laid.

3.   Acts 27:23-24 — An angel appears to Paul on the ship to deliver a message.

C.   **Discerning of Human Spirits**

1.   John 1:47 — Jesus discerns a guileless spirit in Nathanael (compare to John 2:24-25).

2.   Acts 8:20-24 — Peter discerns the wrong motives of Simon the sorcerer.

3.   Acts 14:8-10 — Paul discerns a "spirit of faith" in a lame man (compare to Second Corinthians 4:13).

D.   **Discerning of Evil Spirits**

1.   Luke 13:11-17 — A spirit of infirmity (causing spinal curvation).

2.   Acts 16:16-18 — A spirit of divination (Greek word python) operating through the slave girl.

3.   Revelation 16:13 — Unclean spirits seen as frogs.

III.   **Purpose of the Gift**

A.   **Deliverance From Demons**

Mark 5:5 — *"And constantly night and day, among the tombs and in the mountains, he was crying out and gashing himself with stones."* Also read Acts 8:1-8.

B.   **Reveal the Servants of Satan**

Acts 13:9-10 — *"But Saul who was also known as Paul, filled with the Holy Spirit fixed his gaze upon him and said, 'You who are full of all deceit and fraud, you son of the devil, you enemy of righteousness, will you not cease to make crooked the straight ways of the Lord?'"*

C.   **Expose and Defeat the Work and Utterances of Demons**

Acts 16:16 — *"And it happened that as we were going to the place of prayer, a certain slave girl having a spirit of divination met us, who was bringing her masters much profit by fortune telling."*

D.   **Expose Error**

1.   First Timothy 4:1 — *"But the Spirit explicitly says that in later times some will fall away from the faith, paying attention to deceitful spirits and doctrines of demons."*

2. First John 4:1-3 — *"Beloved, do not believe every spirit, but test the spirits to see whether they are from God; because many false prophets have gone out into the world. By this you know the spirit of God: every spirit that confesses that Jesus Christ has come in the flesh is from God; and every spirit that does not confess Jesus is not of God; and this is the spirit of antichrist, of which you have heard of that is coming and is now already in the world."*

E. Acknowledge and Confess Christ

First Corinthians 12:3 — *"Therefore I make known to you that no one speaking by the Spirit of God says, 'Jesus is accursed'; and no one can say, 'Jesus is Lord,' except by the Holy Spirit."* Also read Matthew 13:13-17.

F. Know the Moving of the Holy Spirit so as to Cooperate With Him

John 3:8 — *"The wind blows where it wishes and you hear the sound of it, but do not know where it comes from and where it is going; so is every one who is born of the spirit."* Also read Ezekiel 37:9-10.

IV. Guidelines for Operating in the Gift of Discerning of Spirits

A. Cultivate the Gift

The gift of discernment can be cultivated by the exercising of spiritual senses. Hebrews 5:14 says, *"But solid food is for the mature, who because of practice have their senses trained to discern good and evil* [spiritual interpretation of what the normal senses show]*."*

B. Test the Spirits

First John 4:1-3 (NIV) — *"Dear friends, do not believe every spirit, but test the spirits to see whether they are from God, because many false prophets have gone out into the world. This is how you can recognize the Spirit of God: Every spirit that acknowledges that Jesus Christ has come in the flesh is from God, but every spirit that does not acknowledge Jesus is not from God. This is the spirit of the antichrist, which you have heard is coming and even now is already in the world."*

C. Examine the Fruit

Matthew 7:16-20 (NIV) — *"By their fruit you will recognize them. Do people pick grapes from thorn bushes, or figs from thistles? Likewise every good tree bears good fruit, but a bad tree bears bad fruit. A good tree cannot bear bad fruit, and a bad tree cannot bear good fruit. Every tree that does not bear good fruit is cut down and thrown into the fire. Thus, by their fruit you will recognize them."*

D.   Not the Gift of Suspicion

This understanding is not to be used in gossip and slander, but rather for edification and helping to cure or mend the Body—not hurt it.

E.   Wisdom, Wisdom, Wisdom!

Wisdom is a necessity. Seek for wisdom beyond your years in the exercising of this explosive gift, and it will be a blessing for you and for the Body of Christ.

F.   Intercede!!!

With this gift may come faith to act or pray with authority. This is usually true of all the revelatory gifts. First, pray your revelation back to the Father and seek His application. After this, you may choose or be guided by the Holy Spirit to release a command to rebuke the enemy discerned; but always pray first for discernment for what to do with your gracelet of distinguishing of spirits.

REFLECTIVE QUESTIONS
LESSON SIX

(Answers to these questions can be found in the back of the study guide.)

FILL IN THE BLANK

1. First Corinthians 12:10 says, "And to another the effecting of miracles, and to another prophecy, and to another the _____ _____ _____."

2. Define in your own words the gift of discerning of spirits. _____

3. List four areas of discernment one may operate in: _____ _____ _____ _____

MULTIPLE CHOICE: CHOOSE FROM THE LIST BELOW TO ANSWER THE NEXT TWO QUESTIONS

A. acknowledge   B. expose   C. know   D. cultivate

4. The purpose of this gift is to _____ the works of satan.

5. The purpose of the gift is to _____ the moving of the Holy Spirit.

TRUE OR FALSE

6. You can cultivate this gift by exercising your spiritual senses. _____

7. There is a tendency with this gift to become critical and judgmental. _____

8. This gift has the capacity to judge whether the spirit operating is human, demonic, or divine. _____

SCRIPTURE MEMORIZATION

9.   Write out and memorize Acts 8:20-24.

PERSONAL REFLECTION

10.   What was the primary point you learned from this lesson?

Notes

SECTION THREE

DREAMS, VISIONS, AND OTHER HEAVENLY REALMS

LESSON SEVEN

DREAM
LANGUAGE

I. Introduction

Dreams are one of the three different avenues of visionary revelation the Holy Spirit uses to speak into our lives. See my book *Dream Language* for full development of this topic. The other two means of visionary revelation—visions and trances—are covered in more detail in the study guide: *Understanding Supernatural Encounters.*

Dreams are closely associated with visions, but dreams, of course, occur during the sleeping hours and visions happen while one is fully awake or conscious. Numbers 12:6 states, *"If there be a prophet among you, I the Lord God will make Myself known unto him in a vision, and will speak unto him in a dream."* While dreams are a specific portion of the prophetic ministry, they are not limited to the prophetically gifted. Joel 2:28 again reveals to us that dreams are a signpost of the Holy Spirit's outpouring: *"And it shall come to pass afterward, that I will pour out My Spirit upon all flesh...your old men will dream dreams...."* It is time for the Church to return to a biblical understanding of dreams as an avenue of discerning God's voice.

II. Biblical Examples of Godly Dreams

A. Dreams to Prophets

1. God spoke in a dream to Abraham (see Gen. 15:12-17), who was a patriarchal prophet (see Gen. 20:7).

2. God spoke through dreams to Jacob (see Gen. 28:12; 31:10), who was also declared to be a patriarchal prophet (see Ps. 105:15).

3. God spoke to prophet Daniel as listed in Daniel chapter 7.

B. **Heathen Received Dreams From God**

1. Abimelech (see Gen. 20:3)

2. Laban (see Gen. 31:24)

3. Midianite (see Judg. 7:13-14)

4. Pharaoh's butler and baker (see Gen. 40:5)

5. Pharaoh (see Gen. 41:7,15-26)

6. Nebuchadnezzar (see Dan. 2:1,4,36)

7. Wise men (see Matt. 2:12)

8. Pilate's wife (see Matt. 27:19)

C. **God's People Who Were Not Prophets Received Dreams**

1. Joseph (see Gen. 37:5,9-10,20)

2. Solomon (see 1 Kings 3:5)

3. Joseph (see Matt. 1:20)

III. **Present-Day Examples of Dreams**

A. **Pastor Gordon**

Boston evangelical preacher — This prestigious minister received a dream of Christ attending his Sunday church service. As a result of this dream, Rev. Gordon radically changed his approach to ministry the rest of his life.

B. **Abraham Lincoln**

It has been noted that President Lincoln was given a dream just days before his assassination concerning his impending death. Perhaps this was used to prepare President Lincoln for eternity.

C. **Eagle Dream of James Goll**

At a critical time in the U.S political history, I was given a dream of a tiring eagle (representative of America) in flight. The question came, "How long will the eagle remain in flight?" The answer proceeded, "As long as the wind is blowing, the eagle will remain in flight!" Let us therefore pray for the winds of the Holy Spirit to continue.

IV.   **Dream Language**

A.   **Dreams Are the Language of Emotions and Contain Much Symbolism**[15]

We must learn to take our interpretations first from Scripture, and then from our own life. God is consistent with His symbolic language. How He spoke in Genesis will be similar to the symbols and types in the Book of Revelation. This holds true in our own life as well.

B.   **Classification of Symbols**

1.   Symbolic actions (see Eph. 2:6; Ps. 10:1; Heb. 10:11-12)

2.   Symbolic colors (see Rev. 3:4-5; 6:2-6; 19:8)

3.   Symbolic creatures (see Rev. 12:9; Gen. 3:14; Luke 13:31-32)

4.   Symbolic directions (see Luke 10:15, 30; Gen. 12:10-13:1; Jer. 1:14)

5.   Symbolic names (see 1 Sam. 25:25; John 1:41-42)

6.   Symbolic numbers (see Luke 10:1; 2 Cor. 13:1; Deut. 19:15)

7.   Symbolic objects (see Matt. 16:18; Ps. 18:2; 1 Cor. 10:4)

C.   **Symbolic Colors**

1.   Amber — glory of God (see Ezek. 1:4, 8:2)

2.   Black — sin, death, and famine (see Lam. 4:8; Rev. 6:5; Jer. 8:21)

3.   Blue — Heaven; Holy Spirit (see Num. 15:38)

4.   Crimson/Scarlet — blood atonement; sacrifice (see Isa. 1:18; Lev. 14:52; Josh. 2:18,21)

5.   Purple — kingship; royalty (see John 19:2; Judg. 8:26)

6.   Red — bloodshed; war (see Rev. 6:4, 12:3; 2 Kings 3:22)

7.   White — purity, light, righteousness (see Rev. 6:2; 7:9; 19:8)

D.   **Basic Principles of Interpretation of Numbers**

Following these principles will help to preserve you from error and extreme.

1. The simple numbers of 1-13 often have spiritual significance.

2. Multiples of these numbers, or doubling or tripling, carry basically the same meaning, only they intensify the truth.

3. The first use of the number in Scripture generally conveys its spiritual meaning.

4. Consistency of interpretation. God is consistent, and what a number means in Genesis, it means through all Scripture to Revelation.

5. The spiritual significance is not always stated, but may be veiled, or hidden, or seen by comparison with other Scriptures.

6. Generally there is good and evil, true and counterfeit, godly and satanic aspects in numbers.

E. Individual Numbers and Their Symbolic Meaning

1. One — God, beginning, source (see Gen. 1:1; Mark 6:33)

2. Two — witness, testimony (see John 8:17; Matt. 18:16; Deut. 17:6)

3. Three — Godhead, divine completeness (see Ezek. 14:14-18; Dan. 3:23-24)

4. Four — earth, creation, winds, seasons (see Gen. 2:10; Mark 16:15; 1 Cor. 15:39)

5. Five — cross, grace, atonement (see Gen. 1:20-23; Lev. 1:5; Eph. 4:11)

6. Six — man, beast, satan (see Gen. 1:26-31; 1 Sam. 17:4-7; Num. 35:15)

7. Seven — perfection, completeness (see Heb. 6:1-2; Jude 14; Josh. 6)

8. Eight — new beginning (see Gen. 17; 1 Pet. 3:20; 2 Pet. 3:8)

9. Nine — finality, fullness (see Matt. 27:45; Gen. 7:1-2; Gal. 5:22; 1 Cor. 12:1-12)

10. Ten — law, government (see Gen. 1; Dan. 2; Exod. 34:28)

11. Eleven — disorganization, lawlessness, antichrist (see Dan. 7:24; Gen. 32:22)

12. Twelve — divine government, apostolic fullness (see Exod. 28:21; Matt. 10:2-5; Lev. 24:5-6)

13.   Thirteen — rebellion, backsliding, apostasy (see Gen. 14:4; 10:10; 1 Kings 11:6)

V.   Inspiration

A.   Dreams May Come From Three Main Sources:

1.   Demonic

2.   Soul

3.   The Holy Spirit

B.   Removing Things From Our Home

There are occasions that we must also remove certain cultic, occultic, or even soulish-tie objects from our home before our sleep will be sweet and clean. Let us cleanse our home in the natural and close all demonic entrances in Jesus' name.

C.   See Deuteronomy 13:1-5

Does the experience lead you into a deeper relationship with the Lord Jesus Christ! We must have more than a profound experience. We must be rooted and grounded in Jesus.

D.   Gifts of Discerning of Spirits

This gift of the Holy Spirit now becomes extremely valuable at this point. We must learn to distinguish what the motivating spiritual force behind certain manifestations, revelations, and experiences is. Let's not be seduced! But let us be wise and cultivate the fear of the Lord and obedience and worship the God of dreams not the dream of God.

(For more on the subject of discerning of spirits see the study guide: *Releasing Spiritual Gifts*. Also study the lesson on "Wisely Judging Revelatory Encounters" found in this study guide to give you a deeper foundation.)

REFLECTIVE QUESTIONS
LESSON SEVEN

(Answers to these questions can be found in the back of the study guide.)

FILL IN THE BLANK

1. Numbers 12:6 (KJV) says, "If there be a _____ among you, I the Lord God will make Myself known unto him in a _____ and will speak unto him in a _____."

2. Dreams come from three main sources. What are they? _____

3. Describe the difference between a symbol and a type: _____

MULTIPLE CHOICE: CHOOSE FROM THE LIST BELOW TO ANSWER THE NEXT TWO QUESTIONS

A. royalty   B. revelation   C. symbolism   D. purity

4. Dreams are the language of the emotions and contain much _____.

5. White as a symbolic color represents _____.

TRUE OR FALSE

6. Dreams are a signpost of the Holy Spirit outpouring. _____

7. Dreams are only given to a select few known as prophets. _____

8. Dreams are important in discerning God's voice. _____

SCRIPTURE MEMORIZATION

9. Write out and memorize Numbers 12:6 and Joel 2:28.

Personal Reflection

10.   What was the primary point you learned from this lesson?

Notes

LESSON EIGHT

LEVELS OF
SUPERNATURAL VISIONS

The following teachings on Levels of Supernatural Visions are inspired from the manual "Understanding Supernatural Visions According to the Bible" by my friend David Castro of Brooklyn, New York.[16]

I. **Spiritual Perception**

A. **John 8:38:** *"I speak that which I have seen with My Father."*

B. **Definition**

In this type of perception, a person possibly sees something in his spirit, but his mind sees no image. The Holy Spirit often shows us things by an unction (see 1 John 2:20). Yet we might not be able to describe those things pictorially. Often a hunch, a prompting, or a "gut feeling" we have is due to a perception in our inner man, which is receiving nudges from the Holy Spirit.

C. **From the Life of Jesus**

Jesus walked by faith and always pleased His Father (see John 8:29). He discerned (saw) the Father's acts (see John 8:38), and He knew (perceived the innermost heart of) all people (see John 2:24-25). It seems that in the life of Jesus, His spiritual eye perceived things that His mind did not always visualize. Such spiritual perceptions could be the operation of the gift of a word of wisdom, word of knowledge, discerning of spirits, or the gift of prophecy. Often the higher the level of Spiritual Vision, the higher the dimension of Spiritual Sight occurs.

II. **Pictorial Vision**

A. **Numbers 12:6:** *"I the Lord will make Myself known unto him in a vision."*

B. **Definition**

In this kind of vision, an image is revealed to the mind and can be identified and described in terms of pictures. Symbols may or may not be involved. Often, the revelatory gifts come to us in the form of pictorial vision. The pictorial vision may also come in a picture superimposed over the subject. You can be seeing two things at once. You may see the main scene with a picture placed over or around it.

C. **Practical Application**

When praying for the sick, an individual may see an image of an organ, a bone, or another body part flash in his mind. This indicates what to pray for or leads to dialogue with the person being ministered to. This is the type of vision being manifested when a Christian is praying for an individual and the Holy Spirit starts showing things in "snap shots." The person may respond by saying, "The Lord is showing me…" or "I'm seeing…" or "I see a vision of…" because pictorial visions are presenting distinct pictures in his mind, and not only in his spirit (as in the case of spiritual perception).

III. **Panoramic Vision**

A. **Hosea 12:10:** *"I have multiplied visions."*

B. **Definition**

In a panoramic vision a person sees a pictorial vision in motion in his mind. This may last a few seconds. You might also hear words in the realm of the spirit.

C. **Biblical Example**

In Acts 9:10-16 we find an example of an internal moving vision. In verse 12, the Lord tells Ananias that Saul had a vision where he *saw* him (Ananias) coming over and ministering to him, though he (Saul) was blind at the time of this vision. This is an account of a panoramic vision. The Greek word used here is *horama*, which means "an entire visible sight." (This Greek word is the root word for the English word "panorama"— *pan + horama*.) Here, Ananias sees a "motion picture" vision instructing him to minister unto Saul (who is later called Paul).

Webster's Dictionary defines "panorama" as "a picture unrolled before the spectator in such a way as to give the impression of a continuous view."

IV. **Dream (Sleeping Vision)**

  A. **Daniel 7:1:** *"Daniel saw a dream and visions in his mind as he lay upon his bed; then he wrote the dream down and related the following summary of it."*

  B. **Definition**

  Here a person receives a message from the Holy Spirit in the form of visionary revelation while asleep. This experience can come in any level of sleep: light rest, regular sleep, deep sleep, or in a trance state. Any one or combination of the revelation gifts may manifest in a dream, with or without symbols, and possibly an entire scenario of a given situation may be shown.

  C. **Scriptural Insight**

  Job 33:14-16 tells us, *"For God speaks once, yea twice, yet man perceives it not. In a dream, in a vision of the night, when deep sleep falls upon men, in slumberings upon the bed; then He opens the ears of men, and seals their instruction"* (KJV paraphrased). God wants to speak to men, but often during the day He can hardly get a word in edgewise. But while men slumber in their sleep, their souls may become rested and more inclined to receive from Him. Then He can open their ears and give them instruction on various levels. Thank God for His persistence!

  (For more teaching and insight on the vast subject of dreams, please see the study guide on *Experiencing Dreams and Visions* and my book *Dream Language*.)

V. **Audible Messages**

  A. **Matthew 3:17:** *"And lo a voice from Heaven."*

  B. **Definition**

Often visions include a voice speaking a message along with a visual image. Sometimes a message is declared apart from any visual pictures. Audible messages in the spiritual realm can involve people speaking words, or objects making sounds. Such messages can be perceived inside of us by our inner ears, or outside of us by our physical ears.

Voices or sounds we hear internally can indeed be messages from the Lord. But that which we hear outside of us—a message from above, and beyond the natural mind and ears—is called a supernatural audible message.

Audible messages from the Lord come in many categories: the Holy Spirit, Jesus, the Father, angels of various realms, and numerous other sounds. (See the lessons on "The Multi-Faceted Voice of God" and "The Inner Voice and Other Leadings" in the study guide entitled *Experiencing Dreams and Visions*.)

Audible voices that are unfamiliar to us and have no visible form may bring doubt and confusion, or even fear. Deceiving or seducing spirits are usually the ones who behave mysteriously, as though they have something to hide (something "up their sleeve"). God is not the author of doubt, confusion, or fear. When God releases His message to us, even through one of His angels, we sense a holiness, a reverence to the Lord, and an openness, because they have nothing to hide.

C. **New Testament Examples**

1. Acts 9:3-7 — Jesus to Saul on the road to Damascus

2. Matthew 3:17 — God the Father to His Son

3. Luke 9:28-36 — God the Father to the disciples on the Mount of Transfiguration

4. Acts 13:1-3 — The Holy Spirit to certain teachers and prophets

5. Acts 8:26 — An angel to Philip

D. **Concluding Thought**

Rest assured! Jesus said that His sheep know His voice (see John 10:15). He is a great teacher, and more than this, He is the greatest Teacher in all of history. He is *the* Teacher. He wants us to hear His voice more than we even want to hear it!

VI. **An Appearance (Apparition)**

A. **Luke 1:11:** *"And there appeared unto him an angel of the Lord"* (KJV).

B. **Definition**

Here a person sees a being who literally appears to him seemingly "out of thin air." The appearance may be seen with the natural eyes open or closed, and it may even be a tangible experience. It may be perceived physically—the being's presence may be felt—without being obviously seen. It is an appearing, a visiting, but not necessarily a sighting.

An apparition is different from a pictorial vision in that it is an actual—perhaps tangible and audible—visitation occurring outside of the person. Whereas pictorial visions, by themselves, are not actual experiences but only revelations with images shown to the mind by the Holy Spirit.

In a pictorial vision, any person, place, or thing (or any combination of these) can be shown to the mind. In an apparition, an object or place does not actually appear to a person, but a person, an angel, or Jesus can. (There could be exceptions to this description.)

C. **Biblical Examples**

1. Joshua 5:13-15 — Joshua saw the Captain of the Lord's army.

2. Acts 10:1-6 — Cornelius saw an angel coming to him with a message.

3. Genesis 32:24-31 — Jacob physically wrestled with an angel.

4. Luke 1:11 — Zacharias saw the archangel Gabriel.

5. Luke 1:26-38 — Mary also saw the archangel Gabriel.

6. Acts 2:3 — The disciples on the day of Pentecost saw the Holy Spirit in the form of "tongues of fire."

7. Acts 1:3 — *"To whom also He showed Himself alive after His passion by many infallible proofs, being seen of them forty days, and speaking of the things pertaining to the Kingdom of God."*

VII. **Divine Sight**

A. **Exodus 3:3:** *"I will now turn aside, and see this great sight."*

B. **Definition**

More than just a spiritual vision, a divine sight is an actual disclosing of a supernatural event. It is like an "appearance" in that it is an actual occurrence outside of the person or persons experiencing it. Only here it is not a being, but an object or activity in the spiritual realm being disclosed to the natural realm.

When Moses was near Mount Sinai, he actually saw a bush burning without it being consumed. This great sighting and this penetrating voice was God in divine manifestation. He conversed with Moses on this holy ground, and commissioned and anointed him to deliver His people Israel from Egyptian bondage.

C.   **Other Biblical Accounts**

    1.   Exodus 19:16-18 — The Lord descended upon Mount Sinai in the form of thunders, lightning, fire, and smoke.

    2.   Exodus 24:9-10 — Moses and the elders saw the Lord with a sapphire pavement under His feet.

    3.   Second Chronicles 5:13-14 — The glory cloud of the Lord filled the temple at its dedication.

    4.   Acts 26:13-19 — A light from the sky which was disclosed in the first heaven shone round about Saul on the road to Damascus at his conversion.

VIII.   **Open Heaven**

A.   **Ezekiel 1:1:** *"The heavens were opened, and I saw visions of God."*

B.   **Definition**

In this type of vision, a hole seems to appear in the immediate sky, the celestial realm is disclosed, and heavenly sights of God become seeable. This is often termed an "open heaven" in historic revivals where the manifested presence of God seems to come down in a tangible manner as conviction of sin, conversions, and healings take place.

C.   **Four Biblical Accounts**

    1.   Ezekiel 1:1-4

Here Ezekiel states that *"the heavens were opened."* He describes a great cloud sent by God to protect him from His brightness. Then he sees flashing lightning, brilliant light, angels, and other details.

2.   Acts 7:55-56

Here Stephen was being stoned to death for preaching the Gospel. As this is occurring, he looked up into heaven and saw *"the sky loosened and the clouds rolled back"* and Jesus standing to receive him.

3.   Revelation 4:1-2

John is now about 80 years old and imprisoned when this experience occurs. He is meditating upon the things of God on the Lord's day. Then he hears a voice and a *"door opened in heaven."* He was then shown the One who sits upon the throne and many detailed messages were received from Jesus.

4.   Matthew 3:16-17

At Jesus' baptism, the *"heavens were opened"* and the Holy Spirit descended upon Him in the form of a dove. Then the Father spoke audibly. *"This is My beloved Son, in whom I am well pleased."*

(For more on this subject, read the last chapter in my book, *The Prophetic Intercessor.*)

IX.   Trance

A.   **Acts 22:17:** *"Even while I prayed in the temple, I was in a trance."*

B.   **Definition**

A trance is a more or less stunned state. In it the person's body is overwhelmed by the Spirit of God, and his mind can be arrested and subjected to the visions or relations He (God) would impart.

The New Testament Greek word for trance is *ekstasis*, from which we derive our English word *ecstasy*. It is basically "a supernaturally incited excitement of the physical body; a being stupefied, held, arrested, and placed in a supernormal (above normal, other-than-normal) state of mind."

Vine's Expository Dictionary of New Testament Words defines a trance as "a condition in which ordinary consciousness and the perception of natural circumstances were withheld, and the soul was susceptible only to the vision imparted by God."[17]

C. **Scriptural Examples**

1. Mark 16:8 — Amazement

2. Mark 5:42 — Astonishment

3. Revelation 1:17 — Falling as dead

4. Daniel 10:7 — A great quaking

5. Job 4:14 — A trembling or a shaking

6. Ezekiel 8:1 — A sudden power

7. Ezekiel 1:3 — The hand of the Lord

8. Job 33:15 and Daniel 8:18 — A deep sleep from the Lord

X. **Out-of-Body Experience**

A. **Ezekiel 8:3:** *"The Spirit lifted me up between the earth and the heaven."*

B. **Definition**

This possibly is an actual projecting forth of the person's spirit and going out or leaving of their body. When God inspires this, He puts a special faith, anointing, and/or protection around the person's spirit so that he can perform what the Lord is leading him into.

When an out-of-body experience occurs, the person's spirit literally leaves his physical body, and he begins to travel in the spiritual dimension by the Spirit of the Lord. Once he is out there, the surrounding environment does not appear the same as it does naturally because now the spiritual eyes are seeing, and not the natural eyes. The Lord directs our eyes to see what He wants us to see, in exactly the way He wants in this unusual experience.

C. **The Experiences of Ezekiel**

1. Ezekiel 3:12-14 — *"The spirit of the Lord took me up…"*

2. Ezekiel 8:1-3 — *"took me by the lock of mine head…"*

3. Ezekiel 11:1-2 — *"the Spirit lifted me up, and brought me…"*

4.   Ezekiel 37:1-4 — *"the hand of the Lord was upon me, and carried me out in the Spirit of the Lord, and set me down in…"*

5.   Ezekiel 43:5-6 — *"So the Spirit took me up, and brought me…"*

D.   A Word of Caution

Counterfeits of all true Holy Spirit-inspired experiences do exist. The difference can be slight and yet very great in its fruit and purpose. We are never to will ourselves into such an experience. This type of experience is only to be God-induced and initiated. It is not self-projection or some rendition of astral projection. When spirits, sorcerers, and yogis practice this without the Holy Spirit and seem to prosper by it, it is because they are not a threat to satan and they are already deceived. Whether they realize it or not, they are already in league with him, and are not his enemies. Do not let the enemy steal what God has ordained. Do not be afraid of these unusual ways of the Holy Spirit and yet do not enter into some type of self-induced activity.

XI.   Translation

A.   Acts 8:39: *"The Spirit of the Lord caught away Philip."*

B.   Definition

Translation (supernatural transportation or translocation) is more properly defined as an actual physical experience, and not just a vision. But when this unusual experience does occur, the individual could be shown various things of the supernatural visionary sort as they are being transported.

C.   Biblical Accounts

1.   Acts 12:8-9 — Here Peter was translated out of prison but while it was happening he did not realize it. As far as he was concerned, he was having a vision or a dream. This could have been some form of translation.

2.   Matthew 4:3-5 — After Jesus was tempted by the devil in the wilderness, He was then transported to another place.

3.   Acts 8:26 — Philip the evangelist was translated after he shared the Gospel with the Ethiopian eunuch.

XII. **Heavenly Visitation**

A. **Second Corinthians 12:2:** *"Such an one caught up to the third heaven"* (KJV).

B. **Definition**

There are three heavens referred to in the Bible. The first, lowest heaven, is the atmospheric sky that encircles the earth (see Matt. 16:1-3). The second, stellar heaven, is what we call outer space, where the sun, moon, stars, and other planets reside (see Gen. 1:16-17). The third Heaven, which is the highest one and the center around which all realms revolve, is Paradise, the abode of God and His angels and saints (see Ps. 11:4).

A heavenly visitation is an out-of-the-body experience, except that here the person's spirit leaves the earth realm, passes through the second heaven, and goes to the third Heaven. This can occur while the person is praying, while he is in a trance or deep sleep from the Lord, or when he dies.

C. **Various Examples**

1. Second Corinthians 12:2-4 — Paul, the apostle, is caught up into the third Heaven where he hears "unspeakable words" and has a truly paradisal experience. Paul seems to have immediately been caught up into this realm.

2. Exodus 24:18; Exodus 25:1,8-9; and Hebrews 8:5 — Possibly this is the type of experience into which Moses entered. We cannot tell for certain. If it was not a heavenly visitation, then it was at least an open heaven where he saw the tabernacle and its blueprint in Heaven. This occurred when Moses was on Mount Sinai in the midst of his 40 days of fasting.

3. Hebrews 11:5 — This tells us briefly of the example of the life of Enoch as recorded in Genesis. He was caught up into Heaven without dying and never returned to earth!

D. **Final Thoughts**

In the same way that a person can visit the third Heaven by having an out-of-body experience, he can also visit the various regions of hell. If he is a sinner, he approaches hell by descending—in death or a near-death experience or in supernatural vision—and shown where he is destined to spend eternity unless he accepts Jesus Christ as his personal Lord and Savior. Then he is brought back to earth and into his body by the mercy of God.

If a person is a Christian, the Spirit of the Lord may bring them to hell in such an experience as well, for the purpose of revealing the suffering torments of the damned. They are then sent back to their body to testify and warn non-Christians to repent and receive Jesus as Lord.

I believe, along with my friend David Castro and other revelatory graced individuals that many people, both in the Bible and throughout history, have had similar experiences, though few are recorded. I believe that these heavenly visitations will be on the increase as true apostolic ministry emerges in these last days. Even so, "Come, Lord Jesus!"

REFLECTIVE QUESTIONS
LESSON EIGHT

(Answers to these questions can be found in the back of the study guide.)

FILL IN THE BLANK

1. A spiritual vision is _____
    _____.

2. A pictorial vision is _____
    _____.

3. A panoramic vision is _____
    _____.

MULTIPLE CHOICE: CHOOSE FROM THE LIST BELOW TO ANSWER THE NEXT TWO QUESTIONS

    A. out-of-body experience   B. open heaven   C. trance   D. divine sight

4. A(n) _____ is an actual disclosing of a supernatural event.

5. A(n) _____ is when one's body and mind is arrested by the Spirit, subjecting him or her to visions.

TRUE OR FALSE

6. Out-of-body experiences are to be God-induced and God-initiated and not self-projected. _____

7. When an out-of-body experience occurs, a person's spirit leaves their physical body and travels in the spiritual dimension. _____

8. A trance is when a hole in the spirit appears and the celestial realm opens up. _____

SCRIPTURE MEMORIZATION

9.   Write out and memorize Ezekiel 1:1; 8:3; and Acts 22:17.

PERSONAL REFLECTION

10.   What was the primary point you learned from Lesson Eight?

Notes

LESSON NINE

THE ECSTATIC REALMS
OF THE SPIRIT

I.   "Trance" Defined

    A.   Webster's Dictionary

        Trance — "ecstasy; a being put out of place; distraction, especially one resulting from great religious fervor; great joy, rapture; a feeling of delight that arrests the whole mind."

    B.   W.E. Vine, Bible Expositor

        A trance is "a condition in which ordinary consciousness and perception of natural circumstances were withheld, and the soul was susceptible only to visions imparted by God."

        "An ecstasy is a condition in which a person is so transported out of his natural state that he falls into a trance, a supernatural state wherein he may see visions in the spirit."[18]

    C.   Greek Definition

        The Greek word for trance is *ekstasis* (from which we get the English word "ecstasy"), and it means: "a displacement of the mind, bewilderment, ecstasy; hence to be amazed, amazement, astonishment."

    D.   Dr. David Blomgren's *Prophetic Gatherings in the Church*

        "A trance is a visional state in which revelation is received. This rapturous state is one in which a prophet would perceptively be no longer limited to natural consciousness and volition. He is 'in the Spirit' where full consciousness may be temporarily transcended."[19]

E.   David Castro, Author, Prophetic Minister

"A trance is basically an ecstatic experience wherein one is more-or-less stupefied, stunned. Herein he is susceptible only to the visions God would impart. If a trance (a deep sleep from the Lord) occurs while the person is already asleep, any of the *visual* or *actual* kinds of supernatural dreams may be experienced. One may see visions, hear words (earthly or heavenly), or he may even leave his body and travel in the Spirit for a special reason. Of course, these things are *not to be self-induced*, but experienced as the Spirit of God wills it."[20]

F.   Vine's Expository Dictionary of New Testament Words

A trance (ecstasy) is "any displacement, and hence, especially with reference to the mind, of that alteration of the normal condition by which the person is thrown into a state of surprise or fear or both."[21]

G.   Other Comments

There are greater and lesser degrees of ecstatic experiences. The New Testament words "amazed," "amazement," and "astonishment" have also been translated from the Greek word *ekstasis*. Hence, we see, both biblically and experientially, there are various degrees of "trances."

One can be shocked, amazed, and joyfully "caught up" in one's emotions due to wondrous activity of the Holy Spirit. Or, perhaps, in a higher level of a trance, one's natural bodily functions are temporarily "put on pause," and the person is caught up in the Spirit (whether in the body or out of the body is not the primary issue), and sees, hears, feels, tastes, touches, or even smells the presence of the Lord in an "otherly" sort of way.

II.   Scriptural Examples Where the Word "Trance" Is Used

A.   Peter's Trance Experience

1.   Acts 10:9-16

"On the next day, as they were on their way and approaching the city, Peter went up on the housetop about the sixth hour to pray. But he became hungry and was desiring to eat; but while they were making preparations, he fell into a trance; and he saw the sky opened up, and an object like a great sheet coming

down, lowered by four corners to the ground, and there were in it all kinds of four-footed animals and crawling creatures of the earth and birds of the air. A voice came to him, 'Get up, Peter, kill and eat!' But Peter said, 'By no means, Lord, for I have never eaten anything unholy and unclean.' Again a voice came to him a second time, 'What God has cleansed, no longer consider unholy.' This happened three times, and immediately the object was taken up into the sky."

2. Acts 11:1-18

Specifically verse 5 is Peter's report at Jerusalem of the trance experience recorded in Acts 10. *"I was in the city of Joppa praying; and in a trance I saw a vision, an object coming down like a great sheet lowered by four corners from the sky; and it came right down to me"* (Acts 11:5).

B. **Paul's Trance Experience**

Acts 22:17-21 says, *"Now it happened, when I returned to Jerusalem and was praying in the temple, that I was in a trance and saw Him saying to me, 'Make haste and get out of Jerusalem quickly, for they will not receive your testimony concerning Me.' So I said, 'Lord, they know that in every synagogue I imprisoned and beat those who believe on You. And when the blood of Your martyr Stephen was shed, I also was standing by consenting to his death, and guarding the clothes of those who were killing him.' Then He said to me, 'Depart, for I will send you far from here to the Gentiles.'"*

C. **Balaam, a Gentile, Old Testament Prophet Who Experienced a Trance**

Numbers 24:4 (KJV) says, *"He hath said, which heard the words of God, which saw the vision of the Almighty, falling into a trance, having his eyes open."*

Balaam is overcome by God's Spirit and he cannot curse, but only bless Israel. This proclamation, while in a trance state, was done while his eyes were open.

III. **Cases Where the Greek Word Indicates They Were "Ecstatic"**

A. **Mark 5:42**

When the witnesses saw Jesus raise the 12-year-old damsel from the dead.

B. **Mark 16:8**

Of Mary Magdalene and others who were with her when an angel of God spoke to them of Jesus' resurrection.

C.   Acts 3:10

Of the people in the temple who saw a lame man healed and praising God.

D.   Luke 5:24-26

"'But in order that you may know that the Son of Man has authority on earth to forgive sins,' He said to the paralytic, 'I say to you, rise, and take up your stretcher and go home.' And at once he rose up before them, and took up what he had been lying on, and went home, glorifying God. And they were all seized with astonishment and began glorifying God; and they were filled with fear, saying, 'We have seen remarkable things today.'"

David Castro says of this passage, "Of the people present here, some were amazed, others glorified God, and the rest were filled with fear. Those amazed were 'entranced' into the spiritual realm where they're yielded and inclined to visions of the Lord; although God probably didn't impart visions to all of them."

Castro goes on to say, "These people were havin' church! They made an effort to come to Jesus' meeting. They came expecting miracles and they were gonna get theirs if they had to break through the wall—and they did! (Talk about bringing down da house!) And as the power of the Lord was present, they got a hold of the realm of the Spirit and went into ecstasy. God could've easily communicated to them by supernatural revelation if He wanted to. Probably some of them were 'slain in the spirit.'"[22]

IV.   **Other Possible Biblical Examples But Where the Word Trance Is Not Specifically Used**

A.   **Abraham in Genesis 15:12**

A state of deep sleep prepared Abraham for God's revelation given to him.

B.   **Ezekiel's Many Occurrences**

1.   Ezekiel 3:14-15 — "*...the Spirit lifted me up and took me away....*" He was transported away to Telabib by the River Chebar.

2.   Ezekiel 8:1-3 — "*...the hand of the Lord God fell on me there. ...and the Spirit lifted me up between earth and heaven and brought me in the visions of God into Jerusalem.*"

3. Ezekiel 11:24-25 — *"And the Spirit lifted me up and brought me in a vision by the Spirit of God to the exiles in Chaldea."* Then he gives the exiles God's message!

4. Ezekiel 43:5 — The prophet is "lifted" up by the Spirit "into the inner court" to "behold the glory of the Lord."

C. Daniel's Many Accounts

1. Daniel 8:15-19, specifically verse 18, *"Now while he was talking with me, I sank into a deep sleep with my face to the ground; but he touched me and made me stand upright."* Daniel fell to the ground and went into a prophetic rapturous state as he went into a "deep sleep."

2. Daniel 10:7-10 — Different versions will state that Daniel had no strength, was deathly pale, helpless, terrified, fell into a deep sleep, or was unconscious as he lay there, face downward.

D. Paul Was "Taken Up" as Cited in Second Corinthians 12:1-4

A clear example of this rapturous trance state was the occasion, as cited by Paul, when a man was "in the Spirit" and caught up to the third Heaven. He states that in his state of trance he was unable to discern whether he was out of the body or in it (see 2 Cor. 12:2).

Note: One does not have to be in a trance to be "in the Spirit." However, one who has had an experience from God of a trance may be properly said to have been "in the Spirit."

E. John the Beloved's Experience

1. Revelation 1:10-18 — Revelation 1:10 says that John was *"...in the Spirit on the Lord's day...."* Verse 17 goes on to state that after seeing the Lord Jesus in His glory, he *"fell at His feet as a dead man."*

2. Revelation 4:1-4 — These Scriptures describe John's summons to *"Come up here...."* John was actually *"in the Spirit"* (Rev. 4:2), because Jesus had called him forth into visions of Heaven. As a result, he was able to behold sights in the third Heaven, and also on the earth.

V.   **These Are Not Mad, as You Suppose!**

There are scriptural references that mention the prophets as madmen or fools. However, a closer study will show that these designations are the contentions of the prophets' critics who assert this of them in mockery.

A.   **Second Kings 9:11**

Jehu has a powerful prophetic word given to him by a young prophet (see 2 Kings 9:1-10). The word states that Jehu will be king and destroy Jezebel. Some called the young man: *"this mad fellow."*

B.   **Jeremiah 29:26**

Often those who prophesy are called madmen.

C.   **Hosea 9:7**

This piercing Scripture describes the view of most toward the *"prophet"* and the *"inspired man."* They are said to be *"a fool"* and *"demented."* These vessels are not fools nor demented. They are truly inspired, God-breathed-upon men and women. These are among those in Hebrews 11's Hall of Fame where it states *"men of whom the world was not worthy."* These are not drunk, or mad, as you suppose! These are inspired men and women of God.

May the Lord grant light, revelation, and understanding to us in these and other wonderful and unusual ways in which a supernatural God works with natural man.

REFLECTIVE QUESTIONS
LESSON NINE

(Answers to these questions can be found in the back of the study guide.)

FILL IN THE BLANK

1. A trance is _____

    _____.

2. Acts 11:5 says, "I was in the city of Joppa…and in a _____ I saw a _____, an object coming down like a great sheet."

3. Acts 22:17-18 says, "When I returned to Jerusalem and was _____ in the temple, that I fell into a _____, and I saw Him saying to me, 'Make haste, and get out of Jerusalem.'"

MULTIPLE CHOICE: CHOOSE FROM THE LIST BELOW TO ANSWER THE NEXT TWO QUESTIONS

A. visional   B. trance   C. prophecy   D. dream

4. A trance is a _____ state in which revelation is received.

5. Numbers 24:4 says, "He hath said, which heard the words of God, which saw the vision of the Almighty, falling into a _____, but having his eyes open" (KJV).

TRUE OR FALSE

6. The Greek word *ekstasis* means a displacement of mind, to be amazed or astonished. _____

7. A trance is not a supernatural state, but merely an excited state of mind. _____

8. A trance can be an ecstatic experience wherein one is stupefied or stunned. _____

SCRIPTURE MEMORIZATION

9.   Write out and memorize Acts 10:9-16 and Numbers 24:4.

PERSONAL REFLECTION

10.   What was the primary point you learned from this lesson?

Notes

SECTION FOUR

INTIMACY: THE GOAL OF ALL THINGS

LESSON TEN

STANDING IN THE COUNCIL OF GOD

The following teaching, Standing in the Council of God, is inspired from the teaching and writing ministry of Carlton Kenney. It is a study concerning the appropriate place for extraordinary spiritual encounters in the life of believers and its special relevancy for the prophetic ministry. Carlton is an excellent Bible teacher and has been a missionary statesman living in Japan over the last quarter of a century.[23]

I.   Introduction

The Lord has revelation—secrets, if you will—that He wants to open up to us. Normally we do not share those secrets with just anyone. Most of us confide the most intimate things only with trusted friends. One of the highest characteristics of a prophetic person is that he or she is supposed to be a trusted friend of God. God has secrets and He is looking for some friends to share His counsel with. It is an open invitation. We all can be friends of God.

II.   Defining the "Council of God"

A.   Theme Scripture: Jeremiah 23:18,22

"But who has stood in the council of the Lord, that he should see and hear His word? Who has given heed to His word and listened?… But if they had stood in My council, then they would have announced My words to My people, and would have turned them back from their evil way and from the evil of their deeds."

B.   **Definition of Council**

1.   From Strong's Concordance: "A session; a counsel of persons in close deliberation."

2.   From Webster's Dictionary: "A group of people called together for discussion, advice; an administrative or legislative body as, a city council; a church assembly to discuss points of doctrine."

C.   **Examples of Deliberation**

1.   Scriptures

   a.   Job 15:7-9

   b.   Psalm 64:2

   c.   Psalm 83:2-3

2.   "The counsel of His will"

   a.   Ephesians 1:11

   b.   Isaiah 40:13-14

D.   **Deliberation Among Intimate Friends**

1.   Scriptures

   a.   Job 19:19

   b.   Psalm 55:13-14

   c.   Amos 3:7

2.   A description

   a.   Revealing in order to get a job done

   b.   Revealing to His friends

E.   **The Circle of Counselors**

1.   Scriptures

   a.   Genesis 49:5-6 — *"Let not my soul enter into their council."*

   b.   Psalm 111:1 — *"In the assembly of the upright."*

   c.   Psalm 89:5-7 — *"The assembly of the saints."*

2. Illustrations

    a. Throne room scenes as in Daniel 7 and Revelation 3 and 4.

    b. Standing in the council equals "being there" as some revelatory people term this experience.

III. A Description of "Being There"

A. In Relation to Our Body

1. Scriptures

    a. Second Corinthians 12:1-4 — *"Whether in the body...or... out of the body."*

    b. Acts 12:9-11 — *"He...did not know that what was done... was real, but thought he was seeing a vision."*

2. In the body — A subjective experience where we are spectating. This could relate to various forms of dreams and visions as in Acts 9:10, 10:3, 15:9, and 18:9.

3. Apart from the body — A subjective experience where we not only spectate, but also interact or dialogue. Possible examples are trances and other experiences as in Acts 10:10, 11:5, 10:19, and 22:17.

4. Out of the body — A subjective experience where we not only spectate, but move about in the spiritual realm. Ezekiel again gives us numerous examples of this in Ezekiel 1:1,3; 3:22; 8:1–11:5,13; 37:1; and 40:1.

B. The Significance of These Experiences

1. There is an honor to God's granting this kind of audience.

2. The more subjective the experience, the greater the possibility of pure revelation. (Remember that these experiences must always line up with Scripture.)

3. During this type of experience, our own thoughts are out of the process and reception in the spirit realm is in clearer focus.

C. Ways to Walk Among Those Standing By

1. Theme Scripture: Zechariah 3:7: *"Thus says the Lord of Hosts, 'If you will walk in My ways, and if you will perform My service, then you will also govern My*

house and also have charge of My courts, and I will grant you free access among these who are standing here.'"

2. Who are those standing by?

    a. Zechariah 1:8-11; 3:1; 4:12-14 — *"These are the ones whom the Lord has sent to walk to and fro throughout the earth"* (Zech. 1:10 NKJV). *"The Angel of the Lord, and Satan standing at his right hand to oppose him"* (Zech. 3:1 NKJV).

    b. Daniel 7:16 — *"I came near to one of those who stood by."*

3. Possible Applications:

    a. Colossians 2:5 — *"For though I am absent in the flesh, yet I am with you in the spirit."*

    b. First Corinthians 5:3 — *"As absent in body but present in spirit."*

4. Three Guidelines or Cautions

    a. Unhealthy familiarity and fascination with their personage:
        i.   Revelation 19:10 — John is tempted to worship the angels.
        ii. Daniel 7:16 — Daniel approaches one standing by, asks questions and receives interpretation of the revelations.

    b. A concern on the issue of "commanding angels" in spiritual warfare encounters. See Matthew 26:53. Jesus says He could make an appeal to His Father and that He would at once put 12 legions of angels at His disposal.

    c. The need for proper discernment in the distinction between the true angelic and the demonic counterfeit.
        i.   All true spiritual warfare centers around the placement of the Son.
        ii.   Luke 10:18 — Jesus said He saw satan falling from heaven like lightning.
        iii. Second Corinthians 2:10-11 — This portrays the necessity of forgiveness so that satan will not be able to take advantage of us.
        iv.   Second Corinthians 11:14 — Even satan disguises himself as an angel of light.

IV. **Factors Pertaining to Standing in His Counsel**

A. **The Hindrance of an Evil Heart**

   1. Sins of prophets

       a. Jeremiah 23:10 — Use their power unjustly

       b. Jeremiah 23:13 — Mixing the source

       c. Jeremiah 23:14 — Engaged in immorality

       d. Jeremiah 23:16 — Speak from their own imagination

       e. Jeremiah 23:17 — Speak peace when there is no peace

       f. Jeremiah 23:24 — Reports are full of falseness

       g. Jeremiah 23:30 — Steal words from one another

       h. Jeremiah 23:32 — Involved in reckless boasting

   2. Balaam's example

       a. Numbers 24:2-4, 15-16

   3. Other Scriptures

       a. Proverbs 3:32 — The crooked versus the intimate

       b. James 4:4-5 — A friend with the world is an enemy of God.

B. **The Fear of the Lord**

   1. The nearness and the remoteness of God

       a. Psalm 139:2 — *"You know my sitting down... rising up."*

       b. Jeremiah 23:23-24 — *"I am a God near at hand."*

   2. Genuine joy of the Lord

       a. Zephaniah 3:4 — *"Take away the filthy garments."*

       b. Jeremiah 23:32 — *"I am against those who prophesy false."*

       c. Isaiah 60:5 — *"Then you shall...become radiant."*

       d. Psalm 2:11 — *"Rejoice with trembling."*

   3. It opens the treasury of God.

       a. Isaiah 33:6 — *"The fear of the Lord is His treasure."*

       b. Psalm 25:12,14 — *"Secret...is with those who fear Him."*

C.   **The Difficulty of Pseudo-Spirituality**

    1.   The problem of identity

    2.   The problem of flawed humanity

    3.   The problem of communication

D.   **Giving Ourselves to the Process**

    1.   Seeking and Finding

        a.   Hebrews 11:6: *"Believe that He is…that He is a rewarder."*

        b.   Genesis 4:25-26: *"For God has appointed another seed."*

        c.   Jeremiah 29:12: *"Then you will call…and I will listen."*

        d.   Second Peter 2:5: *"But saved Noah, one of eight people."*

    2.   Maintaining an objective and subjective experience

        a.   Acts 17:26-27 — *"He has… determined… boundaries."*

        b.   Objective experience — It is not determined by impressions, feelings, inner vision or voices, but is based upon convictions concerning God's character—His faithfulness to keep His promises.

        c.   Subjective experience — The cry of the soul for a clearer awareness of God; the desire for a distinct hearing of His voice.

E.   **Let God Be God!**

    1.   Proverbs 11:3 — *"The integrity of the upright will guide."*

    2.   Psalm 1:6 — *"The Lord knows the way of the righteous."*

    3.   Job 23:10 — *"He knows the way that I take."*

    4.   Isaiah 50:10 — *"Let him trust in the name of the Lord."*

F.   **Four Parameters — Thoughts From Carlton Kenney**

    1.   Face up to our prejudices and return to a biblical position concerning mystical experiences. We must not treat them as weird!

    2.   Let us keep our equilibrium. These experiences are merely a means to an end, not something with which to become overly fascinated.

3. These experiences are a genuine part of the prophetic ministry. The Lord wants to grant richer encounters to all who seek Him. May all of God's people be challenged to a more diligent pursuit of God.

4. Let us provide a friendly climate for emerging prophetic people to mature in their gifting. Now abides faith, hope, and love, these three; the greatest of these is love (see 1 Cor. 13:13). Love is the greatest way for gifts to happen and for ministry to mature. If the church will cultivate a loving environment, then in a few years the church should really get a prophet's reward. May God grant it so!

REFLECTIVE QUESTIONS
LESSON TEN

(Answers to these questions can be found in the back of the study guide.)

FILL IN THE BLANK

1.   The Council of God is _____

     _____.

2.   Ephesians 1:11 (NKJV) says, "In Him also we have obtained an _____,
     being predestined according to the purpose of Him who works all things according to the
     _____ of His will."

3.   Zechariah 3:7 says, "If you will walk in My ways and if you will perform My service, then
     you will also govern My _____ and also have charge of My
     _____ and I will grant you free _____
     among these who are standing here."

MULTIPLE CHOICE: CHOOSE FROM THE LIST BELOW TO ANSWER THE
NEXT TWO QUESTIONS:

   A. wisdom   B. throne   C. revelation   D. son

4.   All spiritual warfare centers around the placement of His _____.

5.   The more subjective the experience, the greater the possibility of pure
     _____. (Remember that these experiences must always line up
     with Scripture.)

TRUE OR FALSE

6.   Forgiveness is a necessity when standing in the council of the Lord. _____

7.   Objective experience is based upon impressions, visions, and voices. _____

8.   Subjective experience is based upon God's character and faithfulness to His promises.

   _____

SCRIPTURE MEMORIZATION

9.   Write out and memorize Jeremiah 23:18,23.

PERSONAL REFLECTION

10.   What was the primary point you learned from this lesson?

Notes

LESSON ELEVEN

HIDDEN STREAMS
OF THE PROPHETIC

I. Introduction

I have found that the most direct road to greater intimacy with God has come through the practice or discipline of something that is almost a lost art in the fast pace of church today—it's called contemplative prayer. Prayer brings us into His presence, and in His presence is the spirit of revelation.

A. An Invitation Was Granted

1. A Dream — "I will reveal the hidden streams of the prophetic to you." This was spoken in a dream from the Lord to me in 1991. This was an invitation from the Holy Spirit into fresh understandings of "old" revelatory ways.

2. A Word — "I will teach you to release the highest weapon of spiritual warfare—the brilliance of My Great Presence." This word came in October 1994 while resting in the Lord.

B. My Personal Journey

As I began to walk in these overlooked pathways in my Christian experience, I found:

1. It was a road less traveled.

2.   The *Desert Fathers* and the writings of others were valuable guideposts for my journey.

3.   Encouragement came from others as I talked with experienced, older saints.

4.   I found it to be a road on which I was already somewhat familiar.

II.   **A Brief Glance at Contemplative Prayer**

A.   **Key Scriptures**

1.   Second Corinthians 3:18 — *"But we all, with unveiled face beholding as in a mirror the glory of the Lord, are being transformed into the same image from glory to glory, just as from the Lord, the Spirit."*

2.   Psalm 46:10 — *"Cease striving and know that I am God; I will be exalted among the nations, I will be exalted in the earth."*

3.   Hebrews 12:2 — *"Fixing our eyes on Jesus, the author and perfector of faith, who for the joy set before Him, endured the cross, despising the shame, and has sat down at the right hand of the throne of God."*

B.   **What Is Prayer?**

There are many types of prayer or focus of prayer. This is not intercession but may lead to it. Prayer is not doing something, but being with Someone. It is communion with God Himself. We are to continue in prayer until we become one with Him. As we continue in "being with Him," we come into a greater "oneness" with Him and eventually an expression of Jesus emanates forth.

C.   **A Synopsis**

We do not intrinsically become Jesus, but when we have set our gaze upon Him (Jesus) (see Heb. 12:2) with loving affection for so long, we become a reflection of His glory (see 2 Cor. 3:18), taking on His character (see Gal. 5:22-23) and His power (see 1 Cor. 12:7-11). A union has taken place in our spirits (see 1 Cor. 6:17), and we have become joined to Him and Him to us. Galatians 2:20 says, *"It is no longer I who live, but Christ who lives in me."*

III.   **What Contemplative Prayer Is Not**

A.   **It Is Not:**

1.   A technique.

2.   A relaxation therapy exercise.

3.   A form of self-hypnosis or mesmerism.

4.   A para-psychological phenomenon.

5.   A "New Age" approach to improve ourselves.

6.   An attempt to make the mind blank or make us "empty-headed."

7.   A "new thing" or a remake of Eastern meditation.

B.   **The Difference Between Contemplative Prayer and Eastern Meditation**[24]

Adapted from a teaching by Dr. Steve Meeks, from Calvary Community Church in Houston, Texas.

1.   Eastern methods are primarily concerned with "awareness." Contemplative prayer is concerned with divine love between God and a person.

2.   Eastern traditions put the greater emphasis on what self can do. Christian tradition recognizes that our unique individuality was created by God and for God as a vehicle for His expression in the world.

3.   Eastern methods seek to get in touch with man's spiritual nature by concentrating on a mantra or some other method of forced concentration. Contemplative prayer presupposes a personal relationship. Contemplative prayer encompasses a voluntary desire to get in touch with our spiritual nature.

4.   Eastern methods focus on what a person can do through focused concentration. Contemplative prayer focuses on surrendering to what only God can do.

5.   Contemplative prayer is not a relaxation exercise, such a breathing techniques or yoga. It is a faith relationship where we open ourselves to our living, personal, loving Father-God.

C.   **Distinctions Between Christian Contemplative Prayer and New Age Thought**[25]

1.   An Overview

The "New Age Movement" appears to be a loosely knit group of individuals and organizations who believe that we have entered a "new age" called the "Age of Aquarius." This age has allegedly replaced the Age of Pisces, which some say represents the Christian era (Pisces — fish — the early Christian symbol). The Age of Aquarius (water bearer) is characterized by humanism, brotherhood and supposed love. It is to be a so-called "golden age." We recognize that New Agers are part of the great counterfeit that may use words, phrases, and techniques that have been borrowed from Christianity and then tainted. Yet, we will not give over either these words or these experiences to be the sole possession of the satanic counterfeit, as they are God's.

For example, New Agers have borrowed "the rainbow" which, of course, was part of God's covenant with Noah. They have stolen the term "centering," which is a word and an experience that has for decades been used by the Christian group, the Quakers.

We have a standard, the Word of God, and our acceptance of a truth is not based on whether or not a counterfeit group has distorted it. We look to see if it is taught in Scripture; and surely such things as the concept of centering and quieting our souls before the Lord are clearly taught and demonstrated by King David in Psalm 62:1,5 where it states, *"My soul waits in silence for God only."*

Therefore, we will expect the New Age to blur the line between truth and error through their eclectic nature. But we shall concern ourselves with encountering fully and completely the God of the authoritative Judeo-Christian Scriptures.

The New Age has arisen to take the territory abandoned by mainstream Christianity. Because Christianity has neglected the initiative and relational and has majored on the propositional and the analytical, a void has been left in the hearts of those who were seeking spiritual encounters. This is certainly no time to draw back from supernatural living and retreat.

Since the dawn of history, whenever people do not preach, proclaim, and model the genuine article, men and women will wander into whatever appears to offer fulfillment of their spiritual quest. We need to cast aside our hesitation and proceed strongly forward with the Word and the Holy Spirit as our unfailing guide!

The New Age is but satan's reaction to the mighty outpouring of the Holy Spirit that we are seeing in this century. I do not see it as something to fear or from which to flee. Since when does light fear darkness? No, I must stand against it in the power of the Holy Spirit and re-claim the land of meditation, contemplation, quietness, revelation, ecstasy, visions, and angelic encounters for His name's sake!

Of course, we need to *"test the spirits"* and confirm every teaching, belief, and practice by the Bible and by the witness of truly godly eldership. But we must remember that there is a fear that comes from satan, and that where this wrong kind of fear is concerned, *"perfect love casts out fear."* We must never allow a "spirit of fear" sent by the enemy to enslave our hearts just because it sometimes masquerades within the church of God under the guise of "appropriate caution" and "respectability."

Let's summarize some of the basic differences between contemplative life under the authority and protection of the Spirit of God as expressed through the biblical Judeo-Christian ethic and contrast it with the illegal abuses and excesses of advocates of spiritualistic New Age heresies.

2.   Nine Basic Tests: New Testament Christianity Versus New Age

   a.   Who is God? — Yahweh, the Lord, the Infinite Personal Creator or a non-personal entity?

   b.   What is the standard of truth? — The Judeo-Christian Bible or evolving, eclectic ancient writings?

   c.   Who is Jesus Christ? — The Only Begotten Son of God or an enlightened teacher, only one of many ascended masters?

   d.   What about salvation? — Purchased by the blood of Christ or the acceptance of the enlightenment that you already are god?

   e.   What is the focus? — Christ-centered or human/self-centered?

   f.   Where is the source of power? — Through Christ or through humanity?

   g.   What is the source of wisdom? — God's divine wisdom or human wisdom?

   h.   The Next Age — Ushered in by God or ushered in by man?

      i.   The stance — Receiving through faith by grace from God or reaching to become gods?

IV.   **A Word of Perspective and Caution**

    A.   **Difficulty in Terms of Description**

        1.   It is one thing to experience the grace of God's imminent nearness; it is another to be able to communicate it. Sometimes someone who truly has a contemplative experience of God expresses it in a way that upsets the more conservative culture of the church and society. Such a person is often labeled a heretic when he is just expressing himself clumsily.

        2.   Mystical language is not necessarily doctrinal, theological language. It is the language of the bedchamber, of love, and hence, hyperbole and exaggeration abound. If a husband says that he adores his wife, it does *not* mean that he regards her as an idol or goddess. He is just trying to express his deep feelings of love in a language that is powerless to fully convey them—except by excessive hyperbole. But if a people in your area do not understand that kind of language, they may think you are under the influence of "another kind of spirit."

        3.   As your contemplative inner experience with God deepens, it may become something about which it will be more difficult to speak. It becomes so precious and sublime that it becomes "holy" to you as it is to God.

    B.   **Caution Signals**

        1.   Maintain a balance between the inner life and the outward, active life of servanthood. Contemplative prayer is meant to bring an enabling into our life of service.

        2.   Spiritual consolation from direct contact with God can be so satisfying that it becomes a trap. You can seek interior prayer for the purpose of escape rather than love. It can become an act of selfish withdrawal rather than of self-surrender.

        3.   Its beauty is so incomparable, its effect so affirming, its power so transforming that it can lead to spiritual gluttony. Beware of just seeking consolation instead of seeking God Himself.

        4.   Use common sense; do not overdo it. Guard the purity of your intentions.

C. **So Now, Let's Proceed!**

Practice does make perfect. Don't just be an armchair coach or theologian. Step out into the cool quiet stream of contemplative prayer, and you will find the great shepherd and lover of our soul—Jesus—who is ready to lead and guide you in your prayer experience.

V. **Contemplative Prayer — Defining Our Terms**

A. **From Webster's Dictionary**

1. *Contemplate* — (1) to gaze at intensely. (2) to think about intensely; to study. (3) to expect or intend; to meditate; muse.

2. *Muse* — to think or consider deeply; meditate.

3. *Meditate* — to plan; intend; to think deeply; reflect.

4. *Reflect* — (1) to throw back (light, heat, or sound). (2) to give back an image (of) mirror. (3) to bring or come back as a consequence; as reflected glory.

5. *Reflect on* (or upon) — (1) to contemplate; ponder. (2) to cast blame or discredit.

6. *Reflective* — (1) reflecting. (2) of or produced by reflection. (3) meditative; thoughtful.

B. **Other Terms Often Used**

1. False Self

This is the "old self" or "old man" (Eph. 4:22-24 NIV), *"You were taught, with regard to your former way of life, to put off your old self, which is being corrupted by its deceitful desires; to be made new in the attitude of your minds; and to put on the new self, created to be like God in true righteousness and holiness."* The "false self" is the ego-centered self life that holds on to and trusts in "false ground" and wrong (untrue) identities wrapped up in whatever possessions or people or power symbols we can lay hold of. The "false self" causes us to cling to other things in order to find happiness, fulfillment, peace, purpose, meaning, and life.

2. True Self

    This is the "new self" or "new man" (Col. 3:9-10 NIV): *"Do not lie to each other, since you have taken off your old self with its practices and have put on the new self, which is being renewed in knowledge in the image of its Creator."* The true self is the "new man" in Christ that we are, become, and continue to put on. Forming the "new man," the true self in God, based on the transforming power of divine love in us, is our participation in the risen life of Christ.

3. Centering

    This is a term from (but not exclusive to) Quaker theology and practice. It simply means to "let go of all competing distractions" until we are truly "present with Him." It is the meditative art of quieting, focusing upon the "center" of all life who lives within the heart (spirit/soul) of each believer in Christ Jesus.

4. Recollection

    It means to bring together into a unified whole. It is allowing the Holy Spirit to cast light upon our fragmentation so as to bring cleansing and healing into our souls (emotions, remembrances, and thoughts).

5. Union With God

    To be made one with our Master and Creator God. It is a work of God upon the heart with two vital preparations from our side of the equation: the love of God and purity of heart.

6. Spiritual Ecstasy

    This is derived from the Greek word *ekstasis*, which is translated "trance" in the New Testament. It is an activity initiated by the Holy Spirit where one is "caught up" into a realm of the Spirit so as to receive those things (revelations, visions, experiences) God desires. It is not an activity we undertake, but a work that God does upon us.

7. A Summary

    After we have worked our way through all the above, the unintelligible language of contemplatives who are struggling to describe the indescribable, we are reduced to the simple confession of Walter Hilton: Contemplation is "love on fire with devotion."

VI.   **Statements From Church Leaders**

A.   **From Richard Foster — Author of *Prayer?Finding the Heart's True Home*[26]**

1.   Contemplative Prayer immerses us into the silence of God. How desperately we in the modern world need this wordless baptism! We have become as the early Church father, Clement of Alexandria, says, "like old shoes—all worn out except for the tongue." Contemplative Prayer is the one discipline that can free us from our addiction to words.

2.   Those who work in the area of spiritual direction always look for signs of a maturing faith before encouraging individuals into Contemplative Prayer. Some of the more common indicators are a continuing hunger for intimacy with God, an ability to forgive others at a great personal cost, a living sense that God alone can satisfy the longings of the human heart, a deep satisfaction in prayer, a realistic assessment of personal abilities and shortcomings, a freedom from boasting about spiritual accomplishments, and a demonstrated ability to live out the demands of life patiently and wisely.

3.   Contemplative Prayer is a loving attentiveness to God. We are tending to Him who loves us, who is near to us, and who draws us to Himself. In Contemplative Prayer, talk recedes into the background, and feelings come to the foreground.

B.   **Ammonas — A Desert Father**

Progress in intimacy with God means progress toward silence. *"For God alone my soul waits in silence"* (Ps. 62:1). "I have shown you the power of silence, how thoroughly it heals and how fully pleasing it is to God…know that it is by silence that the saints grew, that it was because of silence that the power of God dwelt in them, because of silence that the mysteries of God were known to them." It is this recreating silence to which we are called in contemplative prayer.

C.   **Bernard of Clairvaux — 12th-Century Religious and Political Leader in France**

1.   "We felt that He was present, I remember later that He has been with me; I have sometimes even had a presentiment that He would come; I never felt His coming or leaving." (This was Bernard's emotional description of God's loving attentiveness during contemplation.)

2.   In the Christian life we could find, according to Bernard, three vocations: that of Lazarus, the penitent, that of Martha, the active and devoted

servant of the household, and that of Mary, the contemplative. Mary had chosen the "best part" and there was no reason for her to envy Martha or leave her contemplation, unasked, to share in the labors of Martha. In fact, it is unknown for Mary to envy Martha. Contemplation should always be desired and preferred. Activity should be accepted, though never sought. In the end, the completion of the Christian life is found in the union of Martha, Mary, and Lazarus in one person.

D. **Francois de Fenelon — Quietist Leader in France in the Late 1600s and Early 1700s**

1. "Be silent, and listen to God. Let your heart be in such a state of preparation that His Spirit may impress upon you such virtues as will please Him. Let all within you listen to Him. This silence of all outward and earthly affection and of human thoughts within us is essential if we are to hear His voice. This listening prayer does indeed involve a hushing of all outward and earthly affection."

2. "Return to Prayer and inward fellowship with God no matter what the cost. You have withered your spirit by chasing this wish and that wish centered on yourself.

    "Don't spend your time making plans that are just cobwebs—a breath of wind will come and blow them away. You have withdrawn from God and now you find that God has withdrawn the sense of His presence from you. Return to Him and give Him everything without reservation. There will be no peace otherwise. Let go of all your plans—God will do what He sees best for you.

    "Even if you were to alter your plans through earthly means, God would not bless them. Offer Him your tangled mess and He will turn everything toward His own merciful purpose. The most important thing is to go back to communion with God—even if it seems dry and you are easily distracted."

E. **Thomas Morton — Twentieth Century Writer and Priest**

Without the spirit of contemplation in all our worship—that is to say without the adoration and love of God above all, for His own sake, because He is God—the liturgy will not nourish a real Christian apostolate based on Christ's love and carried out in the power of the *Pneuma* (Spirit).

The most important need in the Christian world today is this inner truth nourished by this Spirit of contemplation: the praise and love of God, the longing for the coming of Christ, the thirst for the manifestation of God's glory, His truth, His justice, His Kingdom in the world. These are all characteristically "contemplative" and eschatological aspirations of the Christian heart, and they are the very essence of monastic prayer. Without them our apostolate is more for our own glory rather than the glory of God.

Without contemplation and interior prayer, the church cannot fulfill her mission to transform and save mankind. Without contemplation, she will be reduced to being the servant of cynical and worldly powers, no matter how hard her faithful may protest that they are fighting for the Kingdom of God.

Without true, deep contemplative aspirations, without a total love for God and an uncompromising thirst for His truth, religion tends in the end to become an opiate.

VII. A Description of Contemplative Prayer

A. Contemplative Prayer is an exercise of letting go of the control of your own life by leaning on the props of the false self.

B. It is a kind of communion intended to increase our intimacy with God and awareness of His presence.

C. It is a step of submission where we place our being at God's disposal and request His work of purification.

D. In Contemplative Prayer, we are opening ourselves up to the Holy Spirit to get in touch with our true selves and to facilitate an abiding state of union with God.

E. It is an exercise in learning self-surrender. It teaches us to yield, let go, and not be possessive.

F. It is a method of exposing and disengaging from the ordinary obstacles to our awareness of God's presence with us. This prayer is not an end, but a beginning.

G. It is being still in order to know God (see Ps. 46:10).

H. In Contemplative Prayer, we cultivate the desire to forget ourselves and know God by faith. It is our consent for God's presence and action take over (see Col. 3:10).

I.   It is a movement beyond conversation, a discipline to foster, that leads us into greater faith, hope, and love.

J.   It is an exercise in resting in God. It is not a state of suspension of all activity, but the reductions of many acts to a simple act of saying, "Yes" to God's presence during a time of inner, quiet, devotional prayer.

K.   Contemplative Prayer is the trusting and loving faith by which God elevates the human person and purifies the conscious and unconscious obstacles in us that oppose the values of the Gospel and the work of the Spirit.

L.   It is an activity aimed at fostering the conviction and realization that God lives in us!

M.   This is an exercise in purifying our intentions to desire only one thing: God. It is an act of love. A desire not for the experience of God—but for God Himself.

N.   Contemplative Prayer is a discipline that facilitates not only living in God's presence but out of God's presence. Its transforming effects cause the divine word to once again be incarnated in human form.

O.   Contemplative Prayer is a discipline that enables our developing relationship with Jesus Christ to reach stages of growth in union with God.

VIII.   **Goals and Benefits of Contemplative Prayer**[27]

A.   By means of Contemplative Prayer, the Spirit heals the roots of self-centeredness and becomes the source of our conscious activity.

B.   This prayer helps us to become aware of the presence of God. Living out of that awareness, we gain strength to meet opposition and contradiction without feeling threatened. The continuing awareness of divine love saves us from the need of human affirmation and recognition. It heals negative feelings we have about ourselves.

C.   This form of transforming prayer fosters a different attitude toward one's feelings; it puts them in a different frame of reference. Many of our negative feelings come from a sense of insecurity and the need to build up the empire of self, especially when we feel threatened. But when you are constantly being reaffirmed by God's loving presence, you are no longer afraid to be contradicted or imposed on. Humility will grow as you mature in God's lavish love.

D. This prayer leads us below the conversational level into communion with Him. It basically makes God "more real" to us.

E. As you trust in God and His love for us increases, you are less afraid to have your dark side exposed. We are enabled to "walk in the light as He is in the light and the blood of Jesus cleanses us from all sin." (Truth be known, God always knew the dark side of your character, has loved you all the time, and is now letting you in on His special secret.)

F. The interior silence of Contemplative Prayer brings such a profound cleansing to our whole being that our emotional blocks begin to soften up and our system begins to flush out these poisonous toxins. Bondages may be broken and strongholds destroyed.

G. Although great interior peace may be experienced, this is not the goal. The purpose is not even union with God in a prayer experience. It is to transform us to carry this wholeness with God into the other aspects of everyday life. We are not seeking experiences, but the permanent abiding awareness of being joined to God.

H. Contemplative Prayer will enable us to work for and with others with liberty of spirit because we are no longer seeking our own ego-centered goals but responding to reality as it is with His divine love.

I. Union with God enables us to handle greater trials. God does not make us like Himself in order for us, or Him, to merely look at us! He wants us to do something. Let's release the fragrance of Christ wherever we go.

J. Contemplative Prayer teaches us patience, to wait on God, strength for interior silence, and makes us sensitive to the delicate movements of the Spirit in daily life and ministry.

K. Contemplative Prayer illumines the source and strengthens the practice of all other types of devotions. It gets us in touch with the divine life that is dwelling in us and thus aiding all spiritual disciplines in becoming relational practices.

L. This divine life is actually going on within us 24 hours a day. Much of the time, we do not see it, experience it, or release it. We thus live out of the false empire of self, shutting down the flow of God's divine presence and love.

M. Contemplative Prayer aids us in identifying, experiencing, and releasing His life in and through us as we continue to cultivate the wondrous progression of being immersed into His healing love.

N. As Madame Guyon stated, "This is why God sends a fire to the earth. It's to destroy all that is impure in you. Nothing can resist the power of that fire. It consumes everything. His wisdom burns away all the impurities in a man for one purpose: to leave him fit for divine union."

IX. The Progressive Steps

A. Recollection — Phase One

1. Let go of all competing distractions.

2. Focus not on what has been (guilt, woundedness, etc.) or the future (guidance, words, calling, promises of God not yet fulfilled) but on God in the present tense.

3. Cast our anxieties (cares, worries, fears, tensions) upon Him, for He cares for us! (See First Peter 5:7.)

4. While resting, as the Holy Spirit makes Jesus real to you, close everything off. Picture Jesus sitting in a chair across from you, for He is truly present. God created human imagination. Utilizing your imagination in contemplation is appropriate and one of the best uses by which we can deploy it. This is *not* the same as New Age "imagery and imaging" but simply practicing the presence of God.

5. If frustration and distractions attempt to press in on us, do not follow them (trail after them). But rather, just lift them up into the Father and let Him now care for them.

6. Hear Him say, "Peace, be still." Allow this silence to still our noisy hearts.

7. This centeredness does not come easily or quickly. Being aware of this is even a step in the right direction. Experiencing your inability to conquer these distractions is, as well, another major stride forward.

8. Romano Guardini notes, "When we try to compose ourselves, unrest redoubles in intensity, not unlike the manner in which at night, when we try to sleep, cares or desires assail us with a force they do not possess during the day. Realize, we are not wasting our time. If at first we achieve no more than the understanding of how much we lack in inner unity, something will have been gained, for in some way we will have made contact with the center which knows no distraction."

B. **The Prayer of Quiet — Phase Two**

As we grow accustomed to the unifying grace of recollection, we are ushered into a second phase in Contemplative Prayer, what Teresa of Avila calls, "The prayer of quiet."

We have through recollection put away all obstacles of the heart, all distractions of the mind, all vacillations of the will. Divine graces of love and adoration wash over us like ocean waves. At the center of our being we are hushed. There is stillness to be sure, but it is a listening stillness. Something deep inside us has been awakened and brought to attention. Our spirit is on tiptoe—alert and listening. There now comes an inward steady gaze of the heart sometimes called beholding the Lord. Now we bask in the warmth of His dear embrace.

As we wait before God, graciously we are given a teachable spirit.

Of course, our goal is to bring this contentment into everyday expressions of life. This does not come to us quickly. However, as we experience more and more of an inward attentiveness to His divine whisper, we will carry His presence through our day. Just as smoke is absorbed into our clothing and we carry its smell with us, so the aroma of God's presence is seeping into our being and we will likewise carry His gracious fragrance wherever we go.

C. **Spiritual Ecstasy — Phase Three**

1. The final step into Contemplative Prayer is spiritual ecstasy. This is not an activity or undertaking, but a work that God does upon us. Ecstasy is Contemplative Prayer taken to "the nth degree." Even the recognized authorities in the contemplative life have found it to be a fleeting experience rather than a staple diet.

2. Theodore Brakel — Dutch Pietist in the Seventeenth Century

   "I was transported into such a state of joy and my thoughts were so drawn upward that, seeing God with the eyes of my soul, I felt God's being and at the same time I was so filled with joy, peace, and sweetness, that I cannot express it."

3. Saint Augustine of Hippo — Fourth Century "Doctor" of the Latin Church

   Augustine turned his back on God during his early adult years. But his mother, Monica, who herself came to be known as "Santa Monica" prayed faithfully and earnestly for many years for her son until he finally came into the Kingdom of God. They had an experience on the Tiber River at the city of Ostia.

"They were gazing out a window with deep yearning for God when "with the mouth of our heart we panted for the heavenly streams of Your fountain, the fountain of life." As they were talking, however, words failed them and they were raised "higher and step by step passed over all material things, even the heaven itself from which sun and moon and stars shine down upon the earth. And still we went upward, meditating and speaking and looking with wonder at Your works. We came to our own souls, and we went beyond our souls to reach that region of never-failing plenty where 'Thou feedest Israel' forever with the food of truth. We sighed and left captured there the first fruits of our spirits and made our way back to the sound of our voices, where a word has both beginning and end."

(The subject of trances is covered in detail in the study guide: *Understanding Supernatural Encounters* and the two-tape series, *Trances: A Biblical View*.)

X.   Prayer in the Present Tense

   A.   Poem of Reflection About the Present-Tense God — Helen Mallicoat

> I was regretting the past and fearing the future.
> Suddenly, my Lord was speaking:
> "My name is I AM." He paused.
> I waited. He continued,
> "When you live in the past,
> With its mistakes and regrets,
> It is hard. I am not there.
> My name is not I WAS."
> "When you live in the future,
> With its problems and fears,
> It is hard. I am not there.
> My name is not I WILL BE."
> "When you live in this moment,
> It is not hard. I AM here.
> My name is I AM."

B.   Getting Comfortable With God

Many of us struggle with resting and waiting in God's presence, perhaps because we think He has something against us or we are just to busy. While He calls us into change, He does so by wrapping His arms of love all around us. It takes time before we learn to trust that the best place to be is in our Father's arms. But this will happen. Why? Because He is more committed to the journey than we are!

So come on in and commune with Him. He is waiting for you.

C.   Closing Prayer

"Lord, lead me into these ancient paths, get fresh and vital for today. Teach me Your ways. Silence my fears. Bring me into greater unity with Your Spirit that I might release Your fragrance wherever I go. Amen."

REFLECTIVE QUESTIONS
LESSON ELEVEN

(Answers to these questions can be found in the back of the study guide.)

FILL IN THE BLANK

1. Second Corinthians 3:18 says, "But we all, with unveiled face, _____ _____ as in a mirror the glory of the Lord, are being _____ into the same image from glory to glory."

2. Psalm 46:10 says, "Cease _____ and _____ that I am God; I will be exalted among the nations."

3. Hebrews 12:2 says, "Fixing our eyes on _____, the author and perfector of faith, who for the joy set before Him endured the _____, despising the shame."

MULTIPLE CHOICE: CHOOSE FROM THE LIST BELOW TO ANSWER THE NEXT TWO QUESTIONS:

A. you   B. me   C. sacrifice   D. service

4. Galatians 2:20 says, "It is no longer I who live but Christ who lives in _____."

5. Contemplative prayer is meant to bring an enabling into our life of _____.

TRUE OR FALSE

6. Contemplative prayer is concerned with divine love between God and man. _____

7. Prayer is not doing something, but being with Someone. _____

8. Contemplative prayer is contrary to Eastern mysticism and the New Age. _____

SCRIPTURE MEMORIZATION

9.   Write out and memorize Galatians 5:22-23.

PERSONAL REFLECTION

10.   Ponder, then write down your thoughts about the following questions:

    A.   Am I becoming less afraid of being known and owned by God?

    B.   Is prayer developing in me a welcomed discipline? Express your desires and failures?

    C.   Am I learning to move beyond personal offense and freely forgive those who hurt me?

11.   Reflect on Psalm 42:1-2: "As a deer pants for streams of water so my soul pants for You, O God. My soul thirsts for God, for the living God." Look with your heart and see the panting deer approaching the brook of living waters.

    A.   What are the waters of which your soul thirsts?

    B.   What is the name of the river from which you need to drink?

    C.   What is the stream from which you presently drink?

    D.   Are the waters clear or polluted? Let the Lord now create in you a greater thirst for Him. Then let Him quench that thirst.

12.   What was the primary point you learned from this lesson?

Notes

LESSON TWELVE

THE KEY OF INTIMACY TO OPEN HEAVENS

I.   Introduction

Our desperate need today is to be so hungry for God that we cry out for open heavens to come over our lives, our families, and our cities. We need "Jacob's ladder" to descend again, not just for one night, but permanently (see Gen. 28:11-19).

Let's learn the lessons from Scripture and from past historic revivals as they pertain to "open heavens," and bring forth the necessary ingredients for our day and time. Let us press on to know the Lord Himself and seek Him for the keys that are significant for our day. Truly, intimacy with the Lord is one of the little keys that opens big doors!

II.   Open Heavens From a Biblical Perspective

The following is a brief review of material covered in a previous lesson.

A.   Ezekiel 1:1: *"The heavens were opened, and I saw visions of God."*

B.   Definition

In this type of vision, a hole seems to appear in the immediate sky, the celestial realm is disclosed, and heavenly sights of God become seeable. This is often termed an "open heaven" in historic revivals where the manifested presence of God seems to come down in a tangible manner as conviction of sin, conversions, and healings take place.

C.   **Four Biblical Accounts**

      1.   Ezekiel 1:1-4

      2.   Acts 7:55-56

      3.   Revelation 4:1-2

      4.   Matthew 3:16-17

(For more on this and other related subjects read my book *The Prophetic Intercessor* especially Chapter Twelve.)

III.   **Blowing the Roof Off the House**

A.   **Making Jesus at Home in Your House**

Read Mark 2:1-5 slowly, as a parable. Ask the Holy Spirit to bring personal applications to your life.

      1.   Mark 2:1 — Is Jesus at "home" in your house, family, congregation, city? What would you need to do to have Him be more than the "honored guest" who occasionally shows up?

      2.   Mark 2:2 — When Jesus is "in His temple," people will gather and revelation will rest on the Word of God. May God's house be full to overflowing and may the crowds gather once again to hear the Word of the Lord!

      3.   Mark 2:3 — Some became dissatisfied with the crowds as they were. Four men became desperate for a "break through" on another level. Through the heat of the day, they carried their paralytic friend on a stretcher to the house where Jesus was. They worked hard to carry this "dead weight" possibly quite a distance. It cost them something to get him there, but they wanted more!

      4.   Mark 2:4 — They could not get near Jesus due to the crowds. They could have given up, but instead they moved from the natural into the supernatural to find their solution. Then hope came: "We will tear the roof off the house." So they proceeded up to the rooftop to tear it open with their hands. Through great effort, they dug a big hole in the roof (opened heavens) and lowered their friend into the presence of the living Messiah.

5.   Mark 2:5 — Jesus saw "their faith." Whose faith? All their faith together! Then he spoke to the paralytic: *"Your sins are forgiven."* This results in healing the body.

May these words echo through our lives today and may the sick Body of Christ be raised up to "wholeness."

B.   Opened Heavens Reviewed

1.   Jacob was overwhelmed after his dream, seeing a ladder reaching from earth to Heaven with angels ascending and descending on it (see Gen. 28:11-19). When Jacob lay down to sleep that night, he had no idea where he really was. His dream changed his entire perspective. Once he saw things from God's point of view, his whole outlook changed. He would be the father of a great nation, a man of great wealth and prosperity, but also a man who knew God intimately. We need the gates of Heaven opened over our cities, churches, and families.

2.   Like in Mark 2:1-5, we need to "Blow the Roof Off" our thinking and concepts and believe the Lord for extraordinary works of grace. Desperate times take desperate measures. We need desperate laborers to arise who are not content with life "as is" to tear the roof off in order to lower another into the presence of Jesus!

IV.   People of an Open Heaven

God is looking for candidates in this generation who will be seated with Christ in the heavenly places and call forth God's destiny and design into the earth realm. It has happened before in all historic awakenings. I am talking about ordinary folks who surrendered to an extraordinary God.

A.   Testimony of the Hebrides Island Revival in 1952

Two women, Peggy and Christina Smith, 84 and 82 years old, were desperate for a revival on their island off of Scotland. They began praying from Isaiah 44:3: *"For I will pour out water on the thirsty land and streams on the dry ground; I will pour out My Spirit on your offspring, and My blessing on your descendants."* They reminded God of His word. Then they began to claim Isaiah 64:1: *"O that Thou wouldst rend the heavens and come down, that the mountains might quake at Thy presence..."* (KJV).

The oldest sister was blind, but she received a vision and proclaimed, *"He's coming! He's coming! He's already here!"* The Spirit of God fell in a barn that night where seven young men were praying from Isaiah 62:6-7 where it tells us, *"On your walls, O Jerusalem, I have appointed watchmen; all day and all night they will never keep silent. You who remind the Lord, take no rest for yourselves; and give Him no rest until He establishes and makes Jerusalem a praise in the earth."*

Sure enough God came. This began the great Hebrides Revival under the preaching of Duncan Campbell. A spiritual radiation zone was created and many souls were saved!

B.   Testimony of Evan Roberts and the Welsh Revival of 1904

At the age of 13, young Evan Roberts began to seek the Lord with nightly intercession. At the age of 26, revival came to his hometown in southern Wales. He taught the people to pray two simple prayers. "Send the Spirit now for Jesus Christ's sake." The second prayer was similar. "Send the Spirit now more powerfully for Jesus Christ's sake."

God answered young Evan's prayers and indeed, God's Spirit and tangible presence came down in response as 100,000 souls were swept up into God's Kingdom in a short length of time. Intimacy with Jesus, worship, and intercession were little keys used to shift the atmosphere of a mocking and religious Wales—these keys will be used again in our generation.

C.   Charles Finney — American Evangelist of the 1800s

Charles Finney carried an open heaven with him wherever he went. The anointing on his life was so strong that he would walk into a factory and before he could say a word, people would start weeping and coming under strong conviction of sin. Young and old, male and female all repented of their sins and turned to Jesus. People who came into Finney's presence came under an open heaven, and many, many of them were changed forever.

Today, a cry is arising: "More, Lord!" Yes, there must be a youth revolution come as it was with Evan Roberts. We must have a "trans-generational anointing" as it was with Peggy and Christina Smith. It is time for prayer to arise and to blow the roof off the house!

(Two recommended books for more on this subject: *Revival Fire* by Wesley Duewel and *The Classics of Revival* by Robert Blackhouse.)

V.   When We Care for His Presence

In January 1999 while in a season of rest, the Lord visited me with a piercing dream that set the course of my life and I believe is a clear word to His people.

In this dream, I was holding long loaves of bread, each wrapped in their own individual napkin. I was holding these loaves of bread close to my chest right over my heart. Then I got our youngest child's (Rachel's) blanket, which she has had since birth. I now wrapped these loaves of bread in her dear baby blanket. I held the bread close to my heart and just kind of rocked the bread as you would a newborn child.

Then I heard the words, "When My people will care for, cherish, nurture, and love the "Bread of My Presence" like a parent does its newborn child—then revival will come." I then found myself awakened out of the dream only to find my arms were held out as though holding and rocking something. I then heard myself prophesying out loud in the bedroom the same words I had just heard in the dream as the sweet presence of the Holy Spirit was lingering over my body. The Lord was emphasizing these words by having them be repeated twice!

This I know: He wants us to cherish and care for His presence. Pray for His presence. Love His presence. Nurture His presence. After all, isn't this what you have longed for all your life? Isn't this what you were made and created for: to be a carrier of His most brilliant presence?! Isn't this the answer to the church's cry for help?

When will revival come? You got it! When we get up in the middle of the night, do the night feedings, hold the child close to our bosom, and wash the child of new beginnings with love and compassion—then revival will come! Let His Presence come forth!

VI.   Knocking on Heaven's Door

A.   The Correlation of Revelation 4:1 and Revelation 3:20

The Holy Spirit has been emphasizing Revelation 4:1-3 to many of us around the world for sometime. But as you read these verses you find that it begins, *"After these things I looked, and behold, a door standing open in heaven...."* Much emphasis has been given to the "open door" but less attention has been given to the phrase, *"After these things...."*

I logically and by the spirit of revelation, felt that I must reread the verses that come before Revelation 4:1 and the Holy Spirit led me to Revelation 3:20 and now. Take time to read all these verses. But we will glance at only one in this material, *"Behold, I stand at the door and I knock; if anyone hears My voice, and opens the door, I will come in to him and will dine with him, and he with Me."*

While these wonderful verses have been used effectively over the generations concerning personal evangelism, the historical context of these words both spoken and written are to believers not to unbelievers. These words are written to a church in a city. Do you think that Jesus stands outside the door of the church and that He wants to come in? I do!

I am convinced that there is a door that must be opened in the earthly and natural realm first and Heaven responds to our desperate cry for "More Lord!" and calls us up higher through an open door in the heavens. The key of intimacy open the heavens!

B.   The Summation of All Things!

Intimacy is the key that unlocks open heavens over entire cities. It has happened before and it will happen again. Jesus has been knocking for over 2,000 years. Who is going to answer? Jesus is knocking—patiently knocking—at your door. Do you hear, and will you let Him in?

What is the purpose of *the seer*? Like all seers of old, we must reach high and look heavenward. We must think of others. We must passionately pursue the God of visitation.

All seers must have their aim and focus clear. We must see Jesus! In all our seeing, let's be like John the Beloved. Let's get in the Spirit and release the true prophetic spirit by revealing a testimony of Jesus (see Rev. 10:19). He is the One I long to see. He is the one for whom my heart yearns and pants. He is the goal and prize of my life.

May the key of intimacy be put in the door of our hearts, families, congregations, cities, and nations. May the prophetic power of visions, dreams, and open heavens increase in your life so that you can accomplish the seer's ultimate goal: to reveal Christ Jesus.

REFLECTIVE QUESTIONS
LESSON TWELVE

(Answers to these questions can be found in the back of the study guide.)

FILL IN THE BLANK

1. _____ is the key that unlocks open heavens over entire cities.

2. The seer's ultimate goal is to reveal _____ _____.

3. We must passionately pursue the _____ of visitation.

MULTIPLE CHOICE: CHOOSE FROM THE LIST BELOW TO ANSWER THE NEXT TWO QUESTIONS

A. testimony B. throne C. revelation D. presence

4. When we care for His _____, revival will come.

5. The true prophetic spirit will reveal the _____ of Jesus.

TRUE OR FALSE

6. Open heavens have only occurred in the Bible. _____

7. An open heaven is where the manifested presence of God seems to come down in a tangible manner as conviction of sin, conversions, and healings take place. _____

8. God uses ordinary people to accomplish extraordinary things. _____

SCRIPTURE MEMORIZATION

9. Write out and memorize Revelation 3:20.

PERSONAL REFLECTION

10.   What was the primary point you learned from this lesson?

Notes

Answer Key
for Reflective Questions

Lesson One

1. receptive, communicative
2. Massa
3. Nataph
4. A—*Nabiy'*
5. B—*Ro'eh or Ra'ah*
6. True
7. False
8. True

Lesson Two

1. Answers include dreams and visions, proclamation of God's purpose, heart, or social responsibilities; prophetic worship; prophetic intercession.
2. righteousness
3. seer
4. C—Prophetic intercession
5. D—heart standards
6. True
7. True
8. False

Lesson Three

1. prayed; open
2. have seen
3. Father; Father
4. D—vision
5. B—light

6. True
7. True
8. True

Lesson Four

1. spiritual gifts; gift giver
2. dreams, visions
3. picture
4. C—dreams
5. D—revelation
6. True
7. False
8. True

Lesson Five

1. prophecy; carried or moved
2. be borne along; to be driven along as a wind (see Acts 27:15-17)
3. Holy; human spirit; evil spirit
4. A—glorify
5. D—slavery
6. True
7. True
8. False

Lesson Six

1. distinguishing of spirits
2. Refer to Lesson Six under heading "I. The Discerning of Spirits Defined."
3. discerning the Holy Spirit, angels, human spirits, and evil spirits
4. B—expose
5. C—know
6. True
7. True
8. True

Lesson Seven

1. prophet; vision; dream
2. demonic; soulish; the Holy Spirit

3. *Symbolism* is a representation, one thing standing for another—past, present, or future. A *type* is a prophetic representation, one thing prefiguring something in the future.
4. C—symbolism
5. D—purity
6. True
7. False
8. True

Lesson Eight

1. a seeing in the spirit without the mind seeing an object; may be by unction, hunch, prompting or gut feeling
2. an image revealed to the mind that can be identified and described in terms of pictures.
3. a pictorial vision in motion unrolled before one's eyes
4. A—apparition
5. C—pictorial vision
6. True
7. True
8. False

Lesson Nine

1. a condition in which ordinary consciousness and perception of circumstances are withheld and the soul becomes susceptible to visions imparted by God.
2. trance, vision
3. praying, trance
4. A—visional
5. B—trance
6. True
7. False
8. True

Lesson Ten

1. a group of people called together for deliberation, discussion, council
2. inheritance, council
3. house, courts, access
4. D—Son
5. C—revelation
6. True

7. False
8. False

Lesson Eleven

1. beholding, transformed
2. striving, know
3. Jesus, cross
4. B—me
5. D—service
6. True
7. True
8. True

Lesson Twelve

1. Intimacy
2. Christ Jesus
3. God
4. D—presence
5. A—testimony
6. False
7. True
8. True

APPENDIX A
WISDOM ISSUES DURING TIMES OF REFRESHING

I. **Introductory Statements**

When a fresh breath of the Holy Spirit blows across the church, new and unusual manifestations seem to come with it. Are all the manifestations from God? Are all the experiences biblical? Do these encounters bear fruit that remains? Have people "gone off the deep end" and in the name of freedom and liberty cast off the daily spiritual disciplines? Are these manifestations from God or a human response to God?

All of these, and many more, are valid questions to ask. We must prove all things; hold fast to that which is good. "Time will tell" is a truth that we must always hold fast to. In the midst of new and unusual phenomena, we must be of those who seek the Lord for His wisdom ways. Yet, let's avoid using "wisdom" as a guise or excuse for fear. And at the same time, let's be careful that we don't become offended at what the Holy Spirit is genuinely doing.

II. **Fifteen Wisdom Issues**

A. One of the most important issues is our interpretation of Scriptures—proper exegesis. Many times "prophetically-gifted" people seem to predominantly take a type of loose symbolic interpretation of Scriptures. While there are different schools and methodologies of interpretation, we should look for the historical context from which the Scripture is speaking. One simple wisdom issue is that revelatory gifted individuals perhaps should consult teachers and pastors for greater clarity on scriptural interpretation.

B. Manifestations of or to the Holy Spirit should not take center stage; Jesus is our central focus. While giving ourselves to the purposes of God, movements of the

Holy Spirit, and the current revelatory word from Heaven, let's not jump on "any ol' bandwagon." Avoid fads. Part of the time, we jump into anything that's moving because of our lack of security and proper biblical foundations. Remember, the simple test: does this experience lead us closer to Jesus Christ?

C.   Manifestations are not our primary message. In the mainstream of evangelical orthodoxy, our emphasis is to be the "main and plain things" of Scripture: salvation, justification by faith, sanctification, and then the consequent experiences where people have testimonies of how they are advancing in their relationship with God and the community of believers.

D.   Some things fall into a category of "non-biblical." This does not mean that they are wrong, of the devil, or against the Scriptures. It just means there is no sure biblical text proof to validate the phenomena. Let's not stretch something to try to make it fit. We might not find a Scripture for every manifestation. Let's make sure, though, that we are following the clear principles of the Word of God.

E.   In the times of refreshing, let's keep in focus that there are other sincere believers who are not "as excited about this as we are." This is normal and to be expected. Keep yourself clean from spiritual pride and arrogance. Let's build bridges through love, forgiveness, understanding, and kindness.

F.   Realize that every leadership team of a local congregation has the privilege and responsibility to set the tone of the expression of the release of the Spirit in the congregational gatherings. God does work through delegated authority! Therefore, with hearts and attitudes clean before God, let us pray for those in authority to be given God's timing, wisdom, and proper game plan. Let's be careful when using the label "control spirit" or similar title. Most leaders are sincere believers who are simply trying to do what's best for the overall good of their particular flock.

G.   Is everything and anything supposed to happen all the time? Apart from a sovereign God, I think not. Remember, absolute freedom is absolute nonsense. Ecclesiastes 3:1 tells us, *"To everything there is a season, and a time for every purpose under heaven."* The Scriptures vividly depict "Pentecost meetings." But you will also find admonitions on how to walk with those in the "room of the ungifted or unbeliever" as well. I personally believe it is in line with God's Word to have specific meetings for predetermined specific purposes. The leading of the Spirit works both ways. You can predetermine by His guidance that certain nights or meetings are "refreshing gatherings" as well as "fall into" those spontaneous occurrences when His manifested presence is released.

H. The unusual and rare is not to be the consistent diet or replace the daily Christian spiritual disciplines. If all a person does is "bark like a dog" and quits reading the Scriptures and relating properly to other members of the church, then possibly some other spirit is at work. Perhaps the individual has simply gotten out of focus and needs a word in love spoken to them to help them maintain their spiritual equilibrium in the midst of a mighty outpouring. Whatever the case, let love always be the rule.

I. We must realize that there is no exact science when it comes to figuring out all the manifestations of/to the Holy Spirit. When something is unclear to us, let's not over-define what we don't understand. Realize there is a tightrope of dynamic tension between the reality of subjective experience and biblical doctrine. Let us strive to maintain our balance!

J. Is all of this laughter (crying, shaking, falling, roaring, etc.) from God? I specifically term these "manifestations of/to the Holy Spirit." There is a reason why I term it this way. Yes, some of the external, visible and audible signs are divinely initiated. But we must admit that some of them are human responses and reactions to the Holy Spirit's movement upon us or upon another close by. There is divine initiative followed by human response. This is normal. It's the way it works!

K. While we want to "bless what we see the Father doing," let's also direct this blessing into fruitful works. That is to say, having been refreshed, we now must channel these renewed people into works that would express their faith. Let's channel this energy from a "bless me club" and make it into a "bless others" kind of focus through the demonstration of feeding the hungry, ministering to the poor, the widow, the orphan, and the single parent, evangelism, intercession, worship, and other displays of passion for Jesus and compassion for people.

L. While the phenomena of shaking, laughing, weeping, shouting, falling, roaring, other animal noises, and other bizarre manifestations have occurred in revivals of church history, I doubt that you can make a case for any of these individuals trying to make themselves "roar like a lion." These experiences were equated with receiving an anointing for power in ministry and a tool of radical means whereby God brought personal transformation.

M. What about the fruit of the Spirit of self-control? Have you forgotten it and thrown it out the window? Not at all! Nowhere in the Scriptures are we told that we are to "control God." But we are told to control "self." The fruit of self-control is to conquer the deeds of the flesh. We are to cooperate with the presence of God and control the deeds of the flesh.

N. Let us search Scripture, review church history, seek the Lord, and receive input from those more experienced and wiser than ourselves. The enemy will try to "club Christians over the head" after they've had a renewal and fresh experience so they will become confused, discouraged, and bewildered. Arm yourself. This is a real war. This refreshment isn't just "fun and games." This renewal is to lead us into greater effectiveness for our Master!

O. There are two ditches to avoid. Watch out for analytical skepticism resulting in becoming offended by what you don't understand. The other major negative reaction is one of fear (of man, rejection, fanaticism, etc.). Both of these "ditches" have a common fruit: criticism. Consider the following in regards to a movement or manifestation of the Spirit:

> **"If you can't jump in the middle of it, bless it.**
>
> **If you can't bless it, then patiently observe it.**
>
> **If you can't patiently observe it, just don't criticize it!"**

This is an admonition I received for myself in the past. Perhaps you should consider the warning as well when you find yourself automatically condemning people or things you don't understand.

Appendix B
Interpreting Symbols

I. **Types and Symbols**

    A.   Types are to be viewed as a select group of symbols having prophetic and foreshadowing characteristics.

        1.   Symbol: a representation, one thing standing for another

        2.   Type: a prophetic representation, one thing prefiguring another

    B.   Types are to be viewed as prophetic symbols. This is not to say that all symbols used in prophecy are types. For example: Daniel 7 is prophetic of Gentile kingdoms that are symbolized in this passage as "beasts." These beasts are not types (prophetic symbols), but rather are symbols used in prophecy. A type is prophetic in and of itself and does not depend upon prophetic language for its prophetic import. (For example, Genesis 22 provides us with a type having prophetic import without prophetic language).

- A symbol may represent a thing, either past, present, or future. A type is essentially a prefiguring of something future from itself.

- A symbol is a figure of something either past, present, or future. A type is a figure of that which is to come.

- A symbol has in itself no essential reference to time. A type has inherent in itself a reference to time.

- A symbol is designed to represent certain characteristics or qualities in that which it represents. A type is designed to be a pre-ordained representation of something or someone to come.

- A symbol, to be interpreted, requires a pointing out of the characteristics, qualities, marks, or features common to both the symbol and that which it symbolizes. A type, to be interpreted, generally requires a setting forth of an extended analogy between the type and that which it typifies.

II. **Scriptural Examples**

A. **Symbols**

1. The rock in Psalm 18:2 is a symbol, not a type.

2. The candlesticks in Revelation 1:20 are symbols, not types.

3. The lamb in John 1:29 is a symbol, not a type.

4. The rainbow in Genesis 9:13-16 is a symbol, not a type.

5. The olive trees in Zechariah 4:3 are symbols, not types.

6. The color white in Revelation 19:8 is a symbol, not a type.

7. The number 666 in Revelation 13:18 is a symbol, not a type.

B. **Types**

1. Adam in Romans 5:14 is a type, not a symbol.

2. Animal sacrifices in Leviticus 1–5 are types, not symbols.

3. The offices of prophet, priest, and king in First Kings 1:34 are types, not symbols.

4. The Tabernacle of Moses in Exodus 25–40 is a type, not a symbol.

5. Jonah's experience in the fish in Matthew 12:39-41 is a type, not a symbol.

C. **Types May Involve Symbols, but Symbols—of Themselves—Are Never Types**

1. In Exodus 12, the historical event of the Feast of Passover is a type of Christ and His Church. Within this type there are symbolic elements such as the lamb, the hyssop, the unleavened bread, and the bitter herbs, but these by themselves, are *not* types.

2. In Exodus 17, the historical event of the smiting of the rock is a type of the crucifixion of Christ. Within this type, there are symbolic elements such as the rock and the rod, which by themselves are *not* types.

III. **Conclusion**

The above illustrations show the interrelatedness of types and symbols to be such that, while symbolism may be used in typology, the converse is never true.

ENDNOTES

1. School for Prophecy Lecture Notes (Anaheim, CA: Mercy Publications, 1988), 29.

2. Ibid.

3. Ibid.

4. Quoted in Ern Baxter, *Prophetic Seminar,* teaching notes (Mobile, AL: Integrity Communications, 1984).

5. David Blomgren, *Prophetic Gatherings in the Church* (Portland, OR: Bible Temple Inc., 1979), 27-30.

6. James Strong, *Strong's Exhaustive Concordance of the Bible* (Peabody, MA: Hendrickson Publishers, 1988), "moved" (Greek, #5342).

7. Mark and Patti Virkler, *Communion With God* (Shippensburg, PA: Destiny Image Publishers, 2001), 77.

8. Virkler, *Communion With God*, adapted from a diagram (p. 78) and from a table entitled "Testing Whether an Image Is From Self, Satan, or God" (p. 79). Used by permission.

9. Kenneth Hagin, *The Holy Spirit and His Gifts* (Tulsa, OK: Faith Library Publications, 1974).

10. Dick Iverson, *The Holy Spirit Today* (Portland, OR: Bible Temple Publications, 1976).

11. Derek Prince, *The Nine Gifts of the Holy Spirit*, tape series (Fort Lauderdale, FL: Derek Prince Publications, 1971).

12. David Pytches, *Spiritual Gifts in the Local Church* (Minneapolis, MN: Bethany House Publishers, 1971).

13. John Wimber, *Spiritual Gifts Seminar*, vol. 2, tape series (Anaheim, CA: Vineyard Ministries International, 1985).

14. Francis Frangipane, *Discerning of Spirits* (Cedar Rapids, IA: Arrow Publications, 1991), 6.

15. For the information in this section on the symbolism of colors, numbers, and other items in dreams, I am indebted to Kevin J. Conner and his book, *Interpreting the Symbols and Types* (Portland, OR: Bible Temple Publishing, 1980).

16. David A. Castro, *Understanding Supernatural Visions According to the Bible* (Brooklyn, NY: Anointed Publications, 1994).

17. W.E. Vine, Merrill F. Unger, William White, Jr., *Vine's Complete Expository Dictionary of Old and New Testament Words* (Nashville, TN: Thomas Nelson Publishers, 1996), New Testament section, 639.

18. Ibid, 24.

19. David Blomgren, *Prophetic Gatherings in the Church* (Portland, OR: Bible Temple Inc., 1979).

20. David A. Castro, *Understanding Supernatural Visions According to the Bible* (Brooklyn, NY: Anointed Publications, 1994).

21. W.E. Vine, Merrill F. Unger, William White, Jr., *Vine's Complete Expository Dictionary of Old and New Testament Words* (Nashville, TN: Thomas Nelson Publishers, 1996).

22. David A. Castro, *Understanding Supernatural Visions According to the Bible* (Brooklyn, NY: Anointed Publications, 1994), 47-49.

23. Carlton Kenney, *Standing in the Council of the Lord* (Hampton: Masterbuilder Ministries, 1992).

24. Adapted from the teachings of Dr. Steve Meeks, Calvary Community Church, Houston, Texas.

25. Mark and Patti Virkler, *Communion With God* (Shippensburg, PA: Destiny Image Publishers, 2001).

26. Richard L. Foster, *Prayer: Finding the Heart's True Home* (New York, NY: Harper San Francisco, A Division of Harper Collins Publishers, 1992).

27. Adapted from the teachings of Dr. Steve Meeks, Calvary Community Church, Houston, Texas.

MINISTRY
INFORMATION

If you have benefited from this study guide, James W. Goll has many other study guides available for purchase.

You may place orders for materials from Encounters Network's Resource Center on our Website at www.encountersnetwork.com or by calling 1-877-200-1604.

You may also mail your orders to P.O. Box 470470, Tulsa, OK, 74147-0470. For more information, visit our Website or send an e-mail to info@encountersnetwork.com.

* * * * * * *

Other Books by the Author

Praying for Israel's Destiny
The Coming Prophetic Revolution
The Prophetic Intercessor
The Beginner's Guide to Hearing God
The Coming Israel Awakening

Available from www.jamesgoll.com online resource center or by calling 1-877-22-1604.

DESTINY IMAGE PUBLISHERS, INC.

"Promoting Inspired Lives."

VISIT OUR NEW SITE HOME AT
WWW.DESTINYIMAGE.COM

FREE SUBSCRIPTION TO DI NEWSLETTER

Receive free unpublished articles by top DI authors, exclusive

discounts, and free downloads from our best and newest books.

Visit www.destinyimage.com to subscribe.

Write to: Destiny Image

P.O. Box 310

Shippensburg, PA 17257-0310

Call: 1-800-722-6774

Email: orders@destinyimage.com

For a complete list of our titles or to place an order
online, visit www.destinyimage.com.

FIND US ON FACEBOOK OR FOLLOW US ON TWITTER.

www.facebook.com/destinyimage   **facebook**
www.twitter.com/destinyimage   **twitter**